Jennifer Batten's

ULTRAINTERVALLIC GUITARLICKS

50 Intervallic Licks to Transform Your Rock Guitar Soloing Technique

JENNIFERBATTEN

TRUEFIRE

FUNDAMENTALCHANGES

Jennifer Batten's Ultra-Intervallic Guitar Licks

50 Intervallic Licks to Transform Your Rock Guitar Soloing Technique

ISBN: 978-1-78933-245-2

Published by www.fundamental-changes.com

Edited by Joseph Alexander & Tim Pettingale

www.fundamental-changes.com

Contents

About the Author

The buzz around Jennifer Batten rose from the underground, and guitar magazines promptly began chronicling her savvy musicianship and highly original approach to the electric guitar.

A major turning point came when she was selected from over one hundred guitarists to play in Michael Jackson's highly skilled band, which toured the world for one and a half years, playing for over four and a half million people. In 2012, Sony released an exciting live Wembley Stadium show DVD as part of their BAD 25th anniversary package.

Jennifer wasted no time after the Bad Tour's grand finale, diving into work on her debut album with renowned producer (and ex-Stevie Wonder guitarist) Michael Sembello. Upon the release of *Above, Below and Beyond* in the Spring of 1992, she was again asked to join Michael Jackson for his upcoming Dangerous Tour.

In January '93, she joined Jackson to partake in Superbowl XXVII's half-time entertainment, which aired to one and half billion people in 80 nations. It was the largest audience in television history.

Her follow up CD, *Momentum*, which was heavily influenced by world music, was released just before she left for Michael Jackson's final global tour in support of the HIStory CD in 1997.

In the spring of '98 Jeff Beck asked Jennifer to join his band. They joined forces for three years on the CDs *Who Else* and *You Had It Coming*, which were both supported by world tours. A DVD of this collaboration is available, entitled *Jeff Beck Live in Tokyo 1999.*

Jennifer has authored two music books and released three solo CDs, ranging from World Beat and Rock 'n' Roll, to Electronica. Her CD, *Whatever,* is also accompanied by a 90-minute DVD which includes some of the visuals from her one-woman multimedia show, where she plays guitar in sync with self-made projected films, as well as unreleased music videos and a guitar lesson.

During 2011 she had a guitar residency for the Cirque Du Soleil show *Zumanity* in Las Vegas and recently she has joined forces with **truefire.com** to record instructional videos.

In August 2016 she received the She Rocks "Icon" award and recently was also inducted into Guitar Player Magazine's "Gallery of the Greats".

Jennifer continues to tour the globe in various musical formats, from bands, to solos shows, to clinics and masterclasses.

For more information visit **www.jenniferbatten.com**

Get the Video

Enhance your learning experience!

Thank you for buying this book. To take your learning experience to the next level, we are delighted to be able to offer readers discounted access to the video course on which it is based.

Jennifer Batten's 50 Ultra Intervallic Guitar Licks You Must Know the video course, features 52 multi-angle video lessons with Jennifer. This course is a comprehensive study of Jennifer's intervallic approaches. Work your way through the course and you'll possess an impressive vocabulary of head-turning intervallic licks that you can call on anytime, across the entire fretboard, to spice up your solos and improvisations.

More importantly, you'll gain some solid know-how for crafting your own intervallic lines in any harmonic situation. You'll also majorly beef up your right- and left-hand technique along the way.

For the complete learning experience, head over to **https://truef re.com/fundamental** and use the code: BATTENUP to sign-up for a free account, or scan the QR code below:

Once your account is created, we'll send you a code to purchase the video course at a special price, only available to those who have bought the book.

Introduction

In 1947, Russian musicologist Nicolas Slonimsky published a work called the *Thesaurus of Scales and Melodic Patterns*. It was an exhaustive study of intervallic, melodic patterns designed to provide an endless supply of new ideas for composers. However, many musicians considered the material too heavy and inaccessible, so it was largely ignored for years.

That was until the likes of John Coltrane, Freddie Hubbard, Allan Holdsworth, Frank Zappa, Paul Grabowsky and many other significant artists picked it up and found that it was filled with golden nuggets of information. Each of these musicians has credited Slonimsky's material as a source of great inspiration which, for them, sparked highly creative ideas for improvisation.

Jazz guitar genius Joe Diorio was one of those inspired by Slonimsky's work and he began to write about how he personally applied the ideas. What Joe achieved was to take this intense piece of work and break it down into bite-sized pieces, communicating the material in a way that guitar players could easily understand and apply. He later published his own book, *Intervallic Designs for Jazz Guitar*, focusing on a wide variety of intervallic designs for freestyle improvisation.

I studied with Joe for many years and his ideas really changed my playing. I absorbed Slonimsky's and Joe's intervallic teachings and eventually assimilated those ideas into my own approach for soloing and improvising in a modern rock context. I'll share these ideas with you in this book.

What is an interval?

An interval is simply a name to describe the distance between any two notes, whether that's a half step, a whole step or a larger distance. When I refer to "intervallic playing" in this book, I'm generally speaking about using the bigger jumps, such as 4ths, 5ths, 6ths, 7ths and octaves. These are the intervals that sound a little more unusual and are more challenging to play, as wider intervals demand string skips.

Intervallic playing can open up a whole new perspective on your playing. As soon as you begin to engage with the idea, it opens up the fretboard and produces a flood of new ideas that can make your playing exciting again. Taking an intervallic approach to the scales you *think* you know well can freshen things up.

Often students complain to me that they're playing the same pentatonic patterns and want to break out of it because they're sick of going around the same ideas. Usually I get them to back up at this point and say, "Well, let's stay with the pentatonic scale for a while and see what you can *really* do with it!"

The problem is not with the scale but in how it's applied. We don't have to resort to playing standard rock licks and scale runs, – we can skip strings, use the perfect 4th intervals that occur naturally within the pentatonic scale, create lines with bigger jumps using 5ths or 6ths, and much more.

Using intervallic patterns is a great way to break up a scale and inject some fresh sounds and ideas. It will turn your playing inside-out and enable you to move up to a whole new level. Here, I'll share with you 50 of my favorite intervallic licks to get you started with this style of playing, and I'll show you some ideas that'll help you to develop this style for yourself.

How to use this book

I've organized the material here into eight sections, each of which explores a different tonality:

- In the first section we'll work on the Mixolydian sound that's used over dominant 7 chords
- Next, we'll look at the Aeolian mode or Natural Minor scale over a minor vamp
- We'll also look at the Dorian mode to create a different kind of minor sound
- Then we'll explore the Ionian mode (Major scale) for a major sounding vibe
- Next, we'll work through some intervallic lines for the most evil-sounding tonality, the Diminished!
- Then we'll find some ways to freshen up that old standard, the minor pentatonic
- Intervallic lines can work great over the blues. We'll have worked on dominant chords already, so in this section I've got some great blues turnaround lines for you to learn
- Lastly, we'll get crazy with some altered dominant chord sounds using the Whole Tone scale. I've saved the weirdest stuff till last!

At the beginning of each section, I'll show you some scale patterns to practice. You'll also play through a series of short exercises designed to get you playing and thinking more *intervallically* about each scale.

After that, we'll get into the licks. Along the way, I'll explain the thinking behind each lick, so you can work on your own ideas during practice sessions, and I'll explain any special techniques.

Make sure to download the free audio that accompanies this book, where you'll hear me play each lick several times. You'll also get the backing tracks I used in the audio download, so you can practice the licks on your own and, of course, jam over those vamps to try out your own intervallic ideas. Details of how to get the audio are on the next page.

Get the Audio

The audio files for this book are available to download for free from **www.fundamental-changes.com.** The link is in the top right-hand corner. Click on the "Guitar" link then simply select this book title from the drop-down menu and follow the instructions to get the audio.

We recommend that you download the files directly to your computer, not to your tablet, and extract them there before adding them to your media library. You can then put them onto your tablet, iPod or burn them to CD. On the download page there are instructions and we also provide technical support via the contact form.

Join our free Facebook community of cool musicians and feel free to ask some questions!

www.facebook.com/groups/fundamentalguitar

Kindle / eReaders

To get the most out of this book, remember that you can double tap any image to enlarge it. Turn off "column viewing" and hold your Kindle in landscape mode.

For over 350 free guitar lessons with videos check out:

www.fundamental-changes.com

Join our free Facebook Community of Cool Musicians

www.facebook.com/groups/fundamentalguitar

Tag us for a share on Instagram: **FundamentalChanges**

Chapter One – Mixolydian Licks

About the Mixolydian Scale

All the licks in this chapter are played over an A7 chord vamp and created with the A Mixolydian scale. A Mixolydian is the fifth mode of its parent scale, D Major. It's like playing a D Major scale, but beginning and ending on the note A. The Mixolydian is almost identical to the Major scale, except that the 7th note has been lowered by a half step and this flattened 7th is what gives the Mixolydian its unique color.

A Mixolydian contains the notes: A, B, C#, D, E, F#, G

Although we can relate it back to the D Major scale, it's much better to learn this scale from its A root note and to understand the Mixolydian as a *sound* that has its own unique identity and character. This way, you'll end up playing more meaningful melodic lines that are connected to the chord you're playing over.

Below is the scale shape with its root note on the low E string. Play an A7 chord, then play this shape ascending and descending to help embed the sound of the intervals against the chord in your ears. You'll hear that the scale perfectly fits the A7 chord.

A Mixolydian

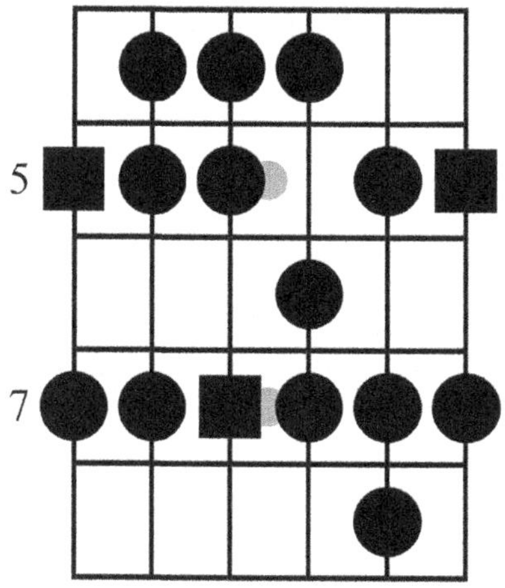

You can work through the CAGED system to play this scale anywhere on the neck, but I'm just going to illustrate one other useful position for you here, which is the A string root pattern in twelfth position:

A Mixolydian

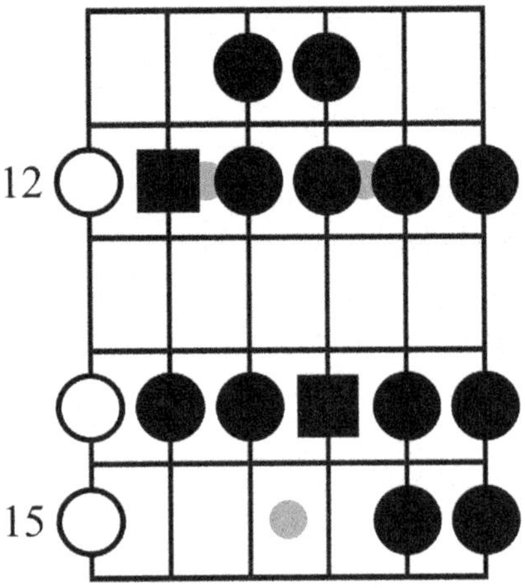

In the above diagram I've included the available scale notes on the low E string to complete the pattern across all strings, but I advise you to always learn and know the scale from the root note. This will make it easier to transfer the pattern to other keys.

Now work through the following series of exercises that'll get you playing this scale in intervals.

We'll start by playing it in 3rds. Although I don't use this sound much in my playing, 3rds are less challenging to the ear than the wider intervals and will ease you into the idea of playing the scale intervallically, rather than sequentially as you're probably used to.

These exercises also help with your fretboard visualization. Your long-term goal is to become familiar with the layout and "geography" of the intervals on the neck.

Example 1a – A Mixolydian in 3rds, ascending and descending

Note that for some intervals, the fingering for the descending pattern will be quite different from the ascending pattern. Work out how to play them in an economical way that's comfortable for you.

Now play through A Mixolydian arranged in 4th intervals.

Example 1b – A Mixolydian in 4ths

The next exercise organizes the scale ascending and descending in 5ths.

Example 1c – A Mixolydian in 5ths

As the intervals get wider, notice that we need to make some adjustments and go beyond the scale's box position shape to avoid any awkward fingering jumps. Here's the scale ascending and descending in 6ths.

Example 1d – A Mixolydian in 6ths

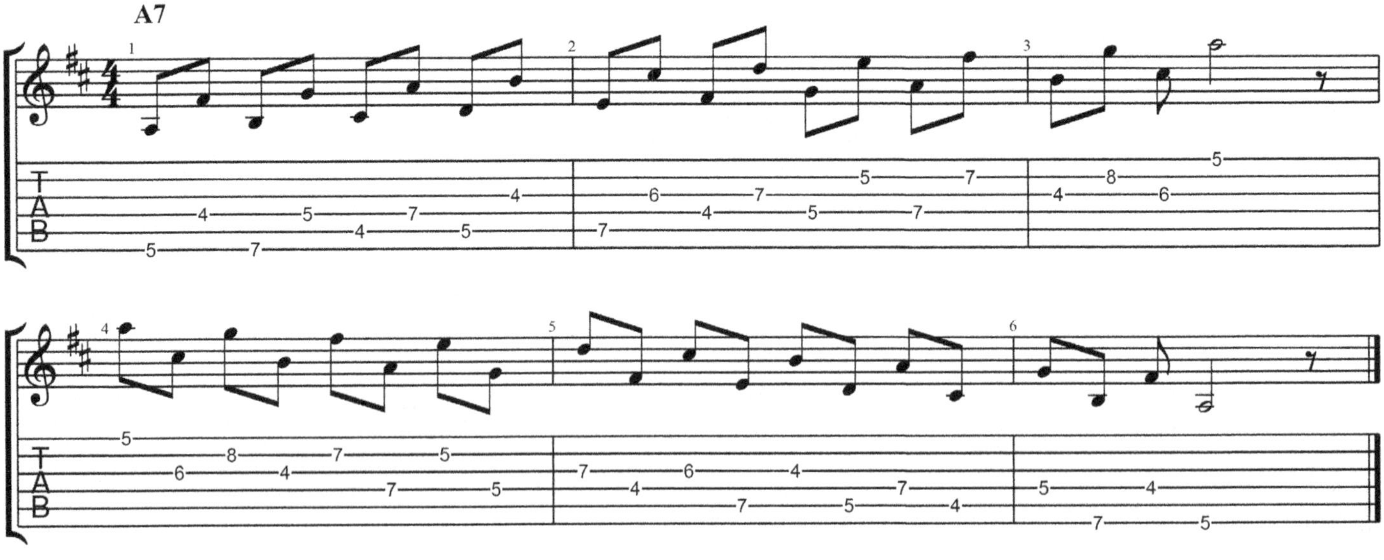

Finally, let's play through the scale in 7ths.

Example 1e – A Mixolydian in 7ths

Continue to work with these patterns during your practice sessions. The more you drill them, the easier you'll be able to pick out any interval with ease. Over time, you'll be able to listen to a piece of music and think, "I recognize that, it's a line in 4ths…" or 5ths or 6ths!

Now let's look at the intervallic licks I've written for you.

I named this first lick *Yoga Stretch*, because I stretch further with my fretting hand than I normally would. Usually, I keep to a one-finger-per-fret approach, but to play this lick it was much more convenient to break out of that pattern briefly into a three-note-per-string (3NPS) shape to line up the series of perfect 4th intervals.

This lick starts with what can be called *interval clusters*, where you ascend by the same interval multiple times. In this example I'm stacking 4ths, which creates a spacious, less diatonic sounding color.

Following the 3NPS pattern, I play the notes at the fifth fret with my first finger, the notes at the ninth fret with my fourth finger, and the notes on the seventh with the second. Bar your finger across the three strings you need to play in each position and use alternate down-up picking.

The lick ends with a descending sequence that spices things up with some half and whole step bends, finishing on the b7 degree of the scale, to highlight the Mixolydian flavor.

Example 1f – *Yoga Stretch*

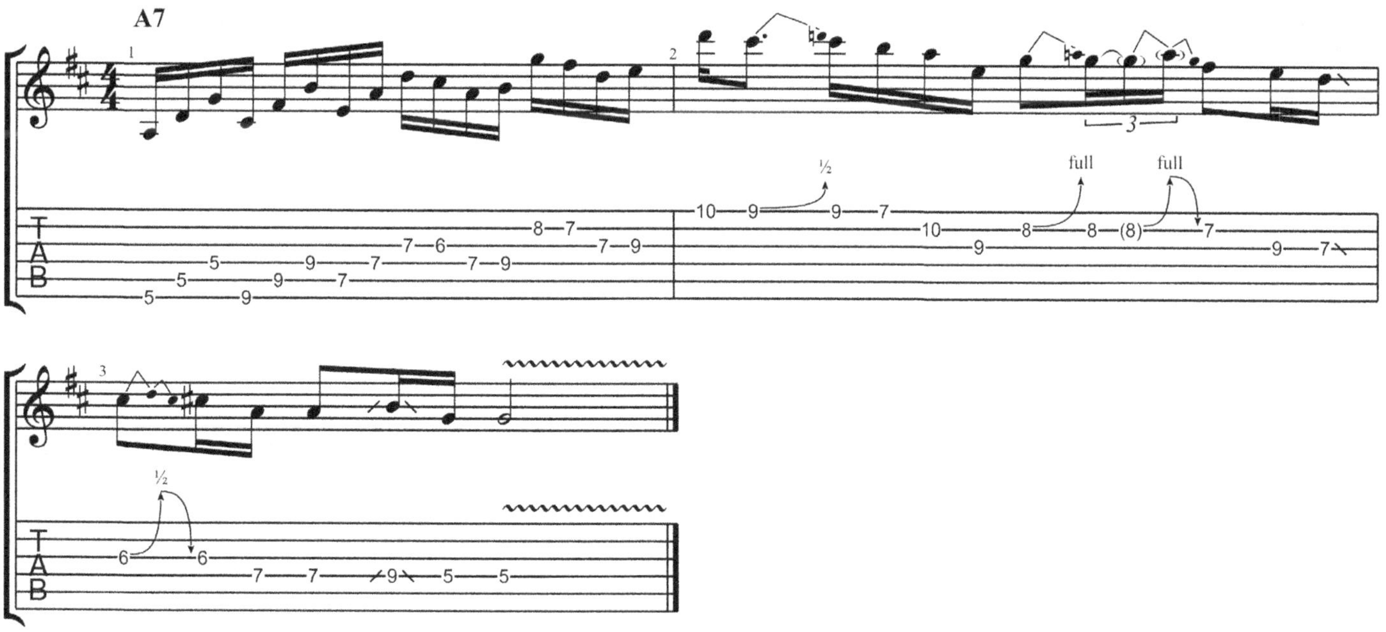

I call the next lick *Bop Not* because it contains an element borrowed from the bebop tradition of jazz. However, it's still played with a Rock 'n' Roll attitude and contains some bluesy bends.

I start by outlining the shape of an A7 chord and the first four notes in bar one come from an A7 arpeggio (played A, E, G, C# in this instance), which is an easy way to define the harmony right at the beginning.

The next four notes form a bebop-like phrase. One of the key ideas of bebop jazz soloing is to target a specific note and approach it chromatically from below or above. Jazz musicians take a lot of liberties with this idea and it always works if the target note is a scale/chord tone that falls on a strong beat.

Here, the target is the E on the D string, 14th fret, which falls on beat 3, and this chromatic lick leads into a stack of 4th intervals.

Bar two contains the bluesy lick that provides some contrast to the angular feel of bar one. The minor to major third bends that occur on beats 2 and 4 are a great way to add in some blues feel to your Mixolydian licks.

Check it out!

Example 1g – *Bop Not*

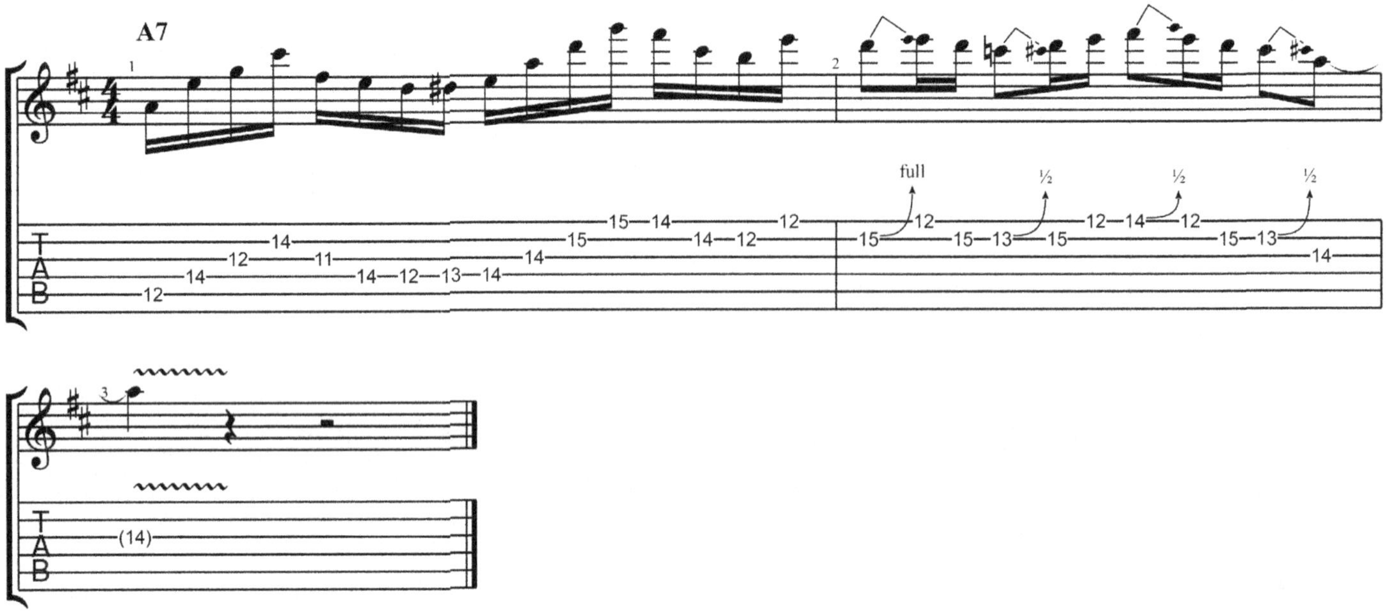

The next idea is called *Skip to my Steve* (rather than *Skip to my Lou*) because I was thinking of Steve Morse's playing style when I wrote it, especially the way he uses chromatic runs in his playing.

Aside from the chromatic passing notes, this lick uses the A Major Pentatonic scale. All these notes are found in the A Mixolydian scale too, but here I opted to use a simpler pattern. As you'll see, the way I break up the pentatonic pattern here is by using string skipping, and this disguises the fact that I'm using a simple scale.

Your goal with a skipping pattern like this should be to focus on picking accuracy and playing cleanly and evenly. The notes are arranged into four-note groups in bar one so practice this as four distinct phrases if you need to, then connect them together.

Bar two begins with two more groups of four before moving into the chromatic ascending lick. Use strict alternate picking for this and hang onto that half step bend at the end of the bar – it's supposed to lag a little behind the beat.

In bar three, I play the A on the B string, 10th fret, with my second finger, with the first finger supporting behind, so I can then slide straight into the bend at the 12th fret.

Example 1h – *Skip to my Steve*

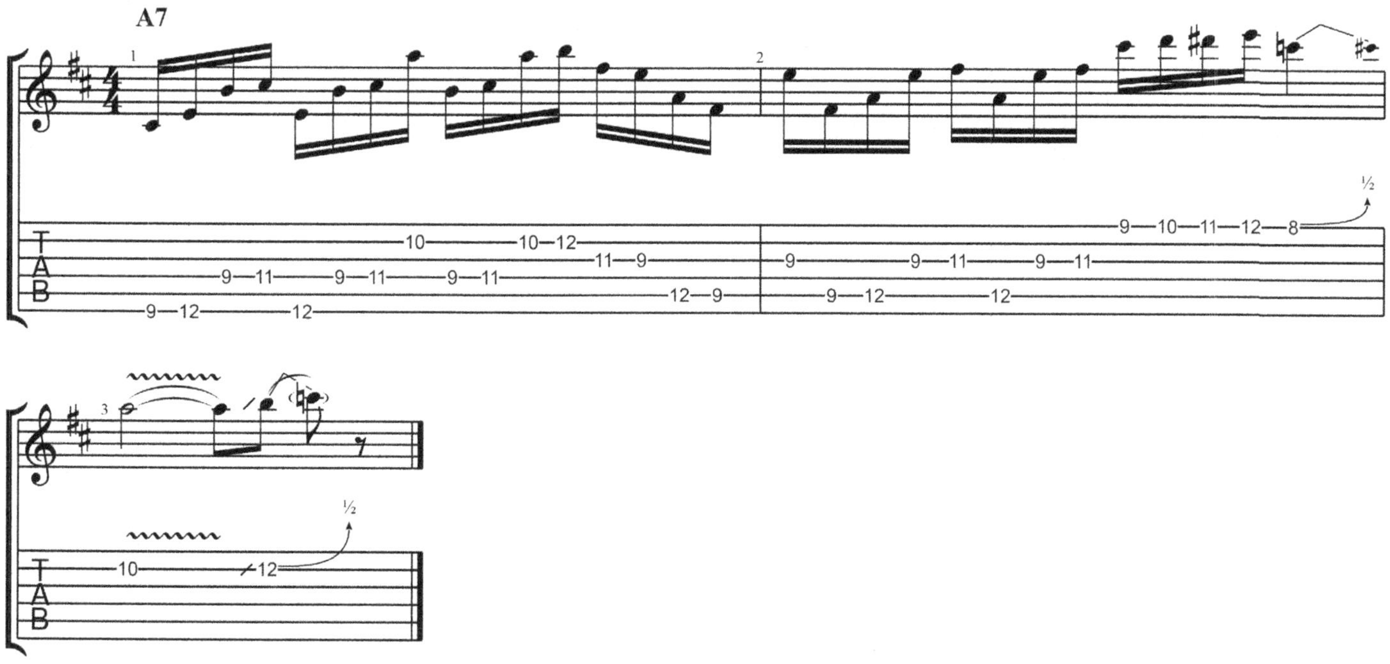

This lick is called *Flat Tire* because I included a flat fifth note in the opening phrase. In the first four-note grouping, the second note (D#) could be explained as a bebop-type chromatic approach note, but I actually chose it deliberately because it's the b5 of the A7 chord we're playing over. Targeting an altered tone is an easy way to achieve tension and resolution or the "outside-inside" sound.

The next four-note grouping is an A7 arpeggio played from the 3rd (C#) and this phrase is repeated an octave higher in the last four-note grouping in the bar.

In bar two, we ground the lick with a descending blues run. It's always good to aim for this kind of balance in a line – intervallic versus bluesy, or angular versus more diatonic sounding. It allows us to keep our audience engaged, while still playing some cool, adventurous lines.

Example 1i – *Flat Tire*

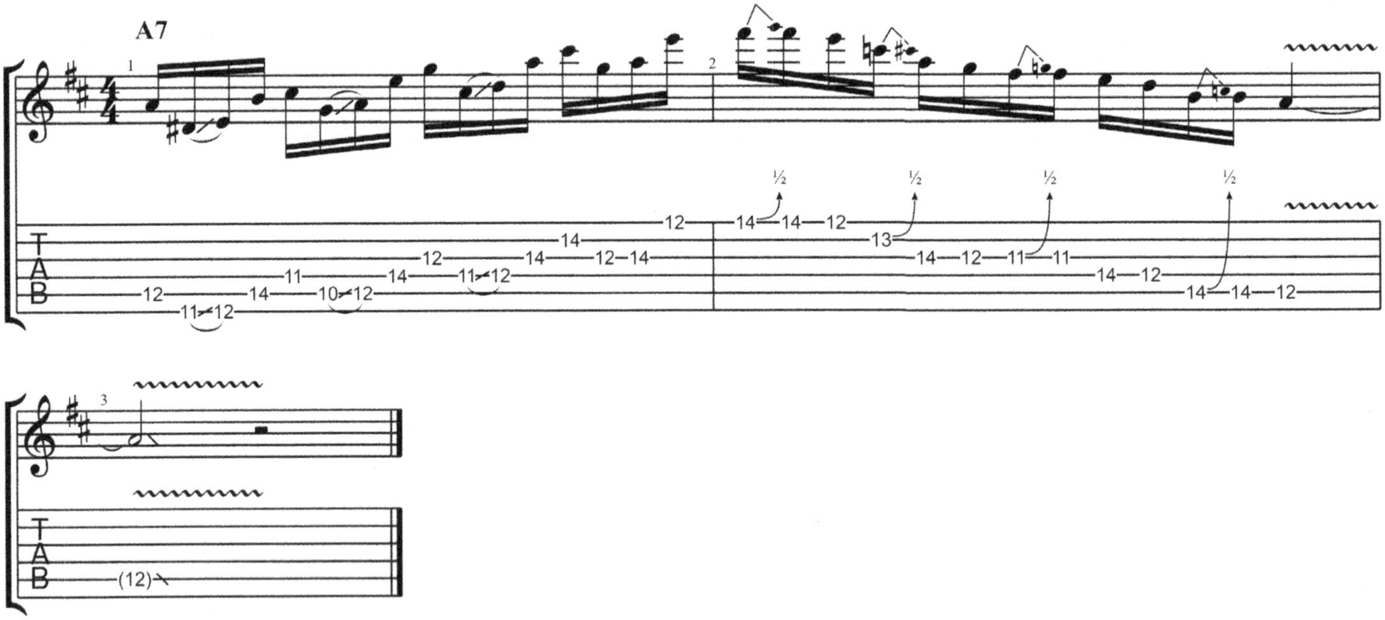

Whenever I hear a tritone lick I always think of Jimi Hendrix, who used this idea so memorably in *Purple Haze* and other tunes.

This lick blends tritone (b5) intervals with perfect 4ths to begin with. Then, like several of the other licks, we bring things home with a blues vibe.

In the opening phrase, the G is followed by a C#/Db (a b5 interval above), and that's followed by another G (a b5 above). These intervals working together produce a distinctive crunchy sound. If you isolate this phrase and play the notes as double-stops for a moment (G and Db together, then Db and G), you'll hear the *Purple Haze* opening lick.

Dominant chords are the ideal vehicle for testing out intervallic ideas, because they can be legitimately altered to contain various tension notes. They are way more forgiving than major or minor chords in this regard!

Example 1j – *Jimi Says*

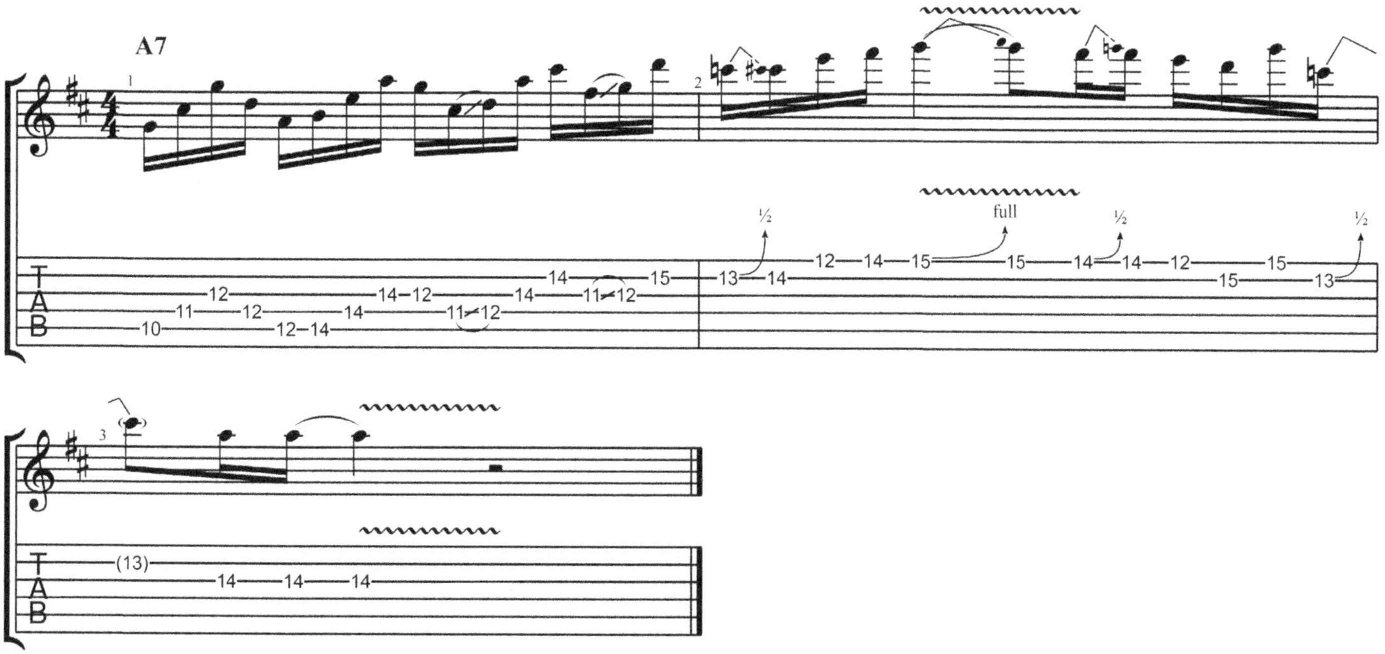

Earlier you practiced playing the A Mixolydian scale in 6th intervals. Now it's time to put these wider intervals to work in *6th Foot Spider* (I challenge you to say it ten times fast).

6th intervals have an incredibly melodic quality – they don't sound as unresolved as 4ths or as ambiguous as 5ths. To play them cleanly, however, requires some fretting hand gymnastics, so walk through this lick before you play it and ensure you finger it in the most economical way.

This is an eight-note sequence that completes nearly two full cycles before being interrupted with a bluesy closing statement.

Instead of using continually ascending 6ths, I chose to combine ascending and descending movements to stop the lick from sounding too predictable. We don't want to exhaust the sound of the interval. The pattern being used is ascend, descend, ascend, ascend.

This will challenge your alternate picking so be sure to be careful of unwanted string noise when skipping strings.

Example 1k – *6th Foot Spider*

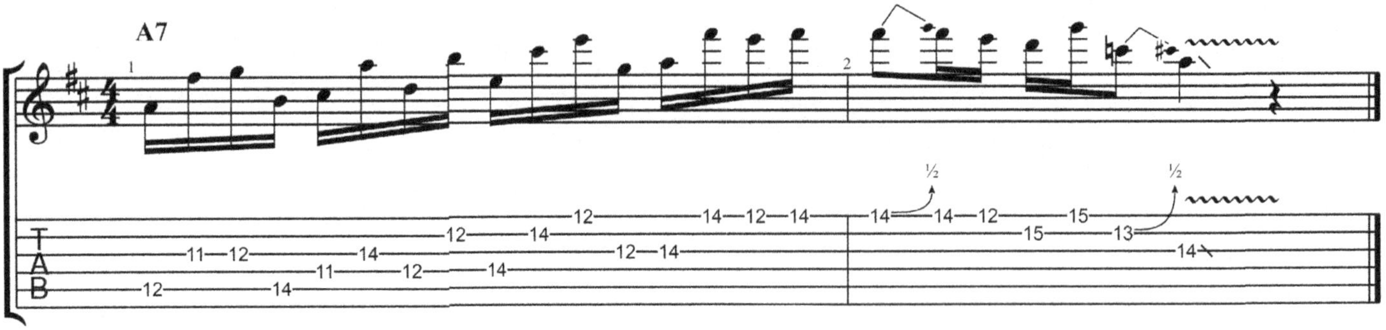

The next example uses unison notes. The guitar is one of the few instruments where you can play the same note in several different places. The great thing about this is that unison notes sound slightly different in each location because of the change in timbre.

The lick begins with the root, 5th and 9th scale tones. (Throughout this book you'll discover that I love this 1-5-9 sound and use it quite a bit). Then, the 9th is repeated as a unison note on a different string. The line continues into a series of perfect and flat 5th intervals and 4ths before landing on the major 3rd scale tone.

You'll have heard the sound of 1-5-9 used by Andy Summers to craft memorable riffs for *The Police* on tunes like *Message in a Bottle* and *Every Breath You Take.*

Example 1l – *Unison Face*

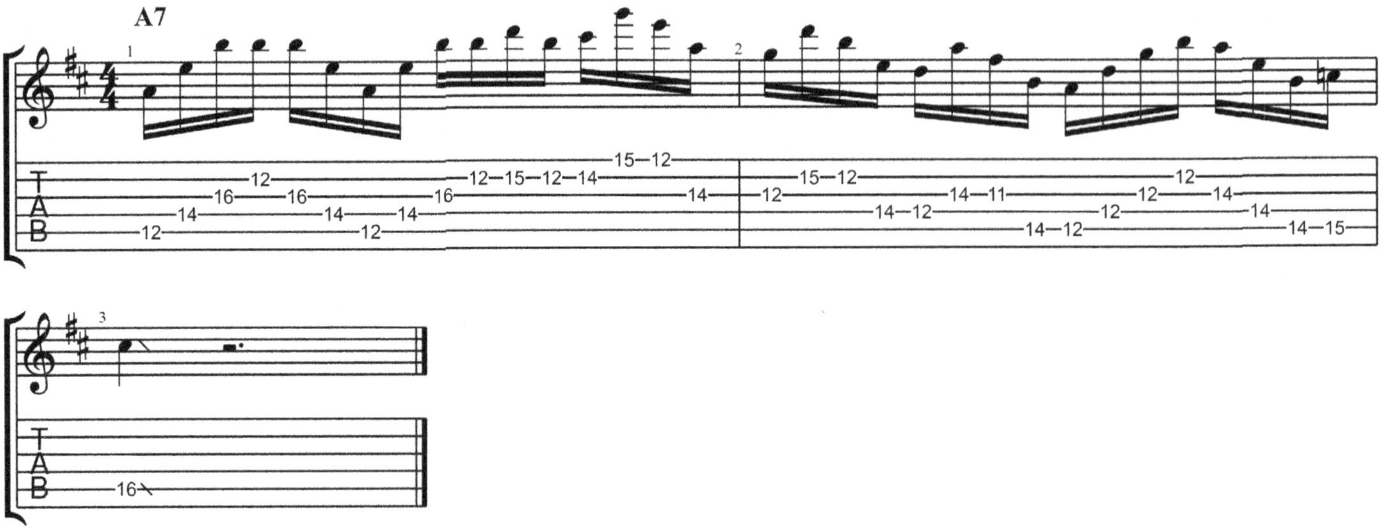

Our final Mixolydian intervallic lick slides all over the fretboard (hence the name *Rollerbladin'*) using pairs of stacked 5ths from different degrees of the Mixolydian scale. It's all about taking an intervallic shape (root, 5th and 9th again) and moving it up the fretboard.

The big difference between this lick and the previous one is how I map out the 5ths on the fretboard. Previously we used a five-fret spread from the 12th to the 16th fret, but this stretch becomes increasingly difficult to negotiate as you move down the fretboard. We can play a much more manageable fingering with the help of some cunning string skips.

This is another example of how knowing your fretboard and using alternate fingerings can expand your melodic potential.

Example 1m – *Rollerbladin'*

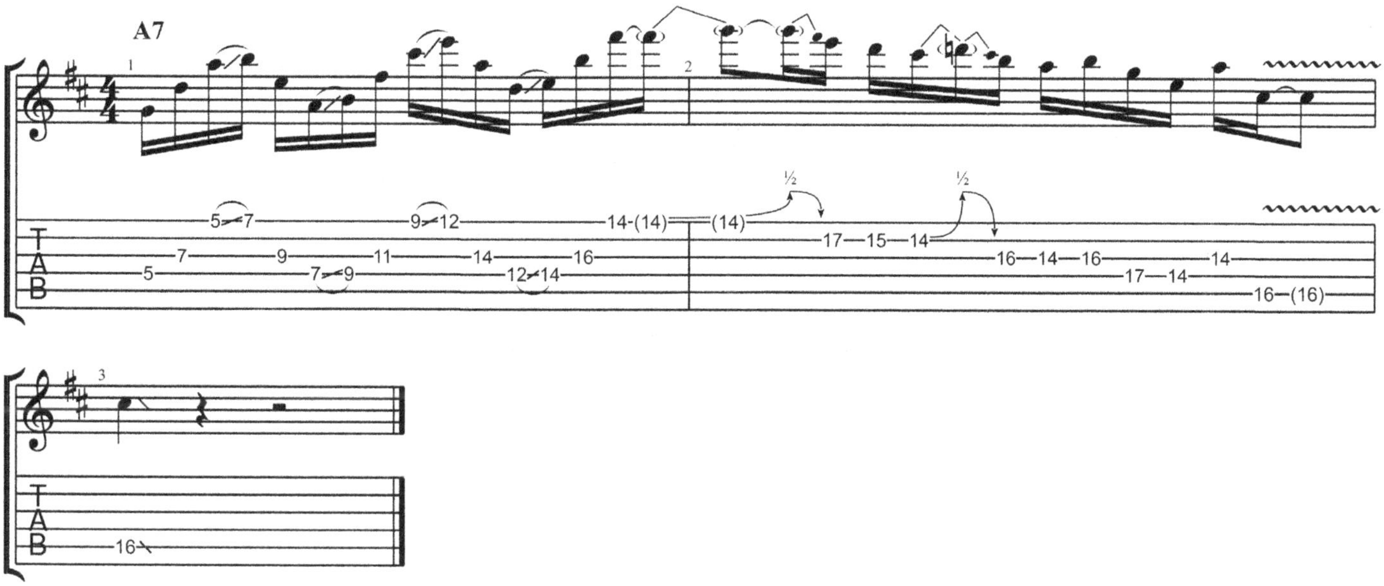

Chapter Two – Aeolian Licks

About the Aeolian Scale

All the licks in this chapter are played over a Cm7 chord vamp using the C Aeolian scale which is the sixth mode of its parent scale, Eb Major. Aeolian is also known as the Natural Minor scale and is the *relative minor* to its major parent scale.

C Aeolian contains the notes: C, D, Eb, F, G, Ab, Bb.

Within it, it also contains the C Minor Pentatonic scale (C, Eb, F, G, Bb), so if we want to limit ourselves (in a good way) and make the most of just a few notes, this minor pentatonic is a good option.

Below is the E string root shape for the scale in eighth position. Play a Cm7 chord, then play this shape ascending and descending and hear how it interacts with the chord.

C Aeolian

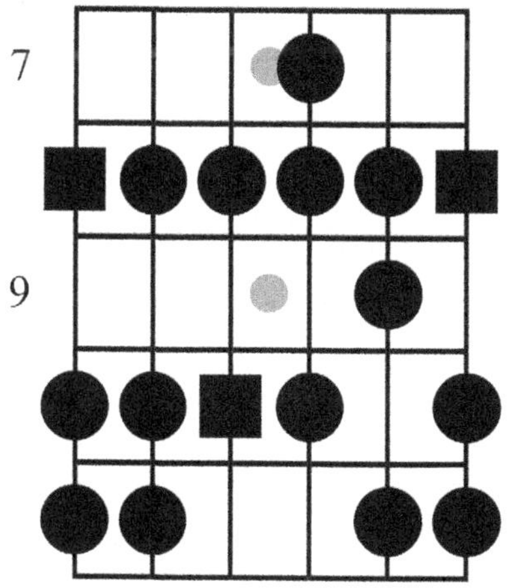

Now, here's C Aeolian in third position, with the root note on the A string.

C Aeolian

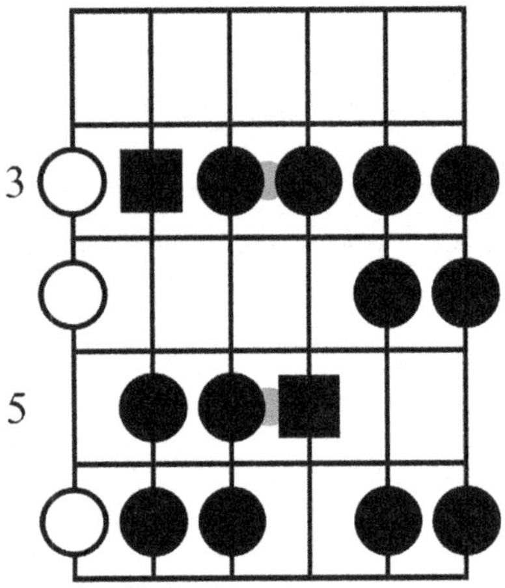

Aeolian is the mode that most people tend to learn first, along with the Ionian (Major scale), because of their strong harmonic relationship. It's perhaps the most obvious minor sound to reach for when playing over a minor vamp, but that doesn't mean it has to sound boring.

As in the previous chapter, here are some exercises to help you practice navigating the scale in wider intervals. They are designed to embed the sound of the scale in your ears and also your muscle memory, so don't miss these out and skip right to the licks – this training is an essential part of the journey.

For the first exercise, this time we'll dive straight in and play the scale in 4ths, ascending and descending.

Example 2a

Now let's break the scale into 5th intervals.

Example 2b

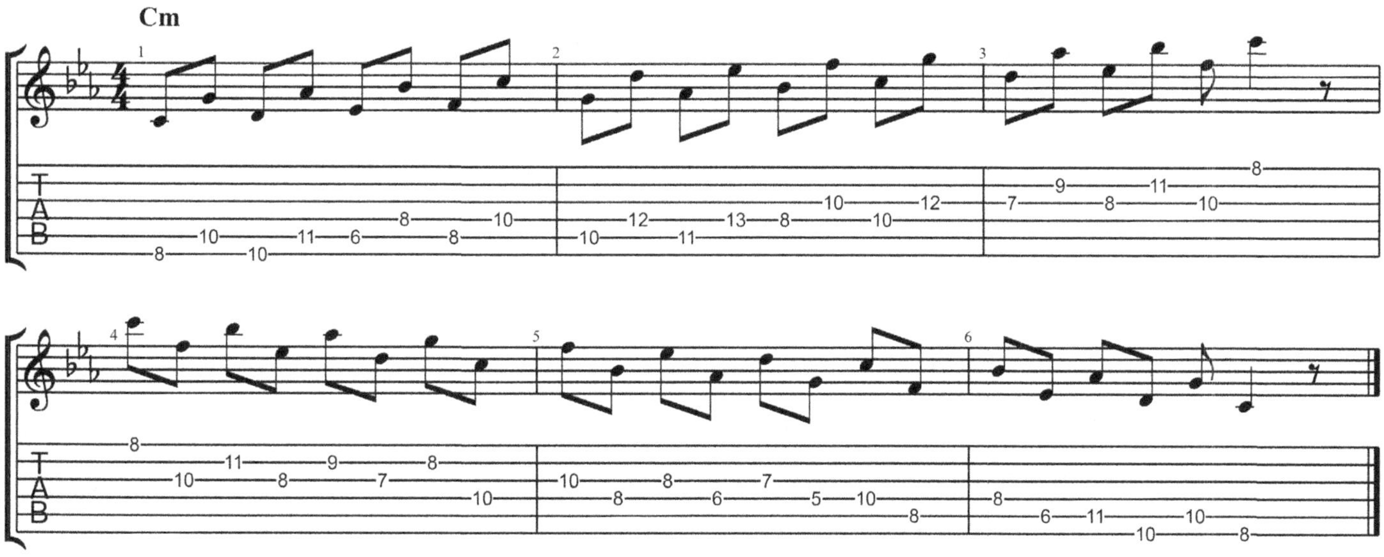

And finally, play through it in 6ths, ascending and descending.

Example 2c

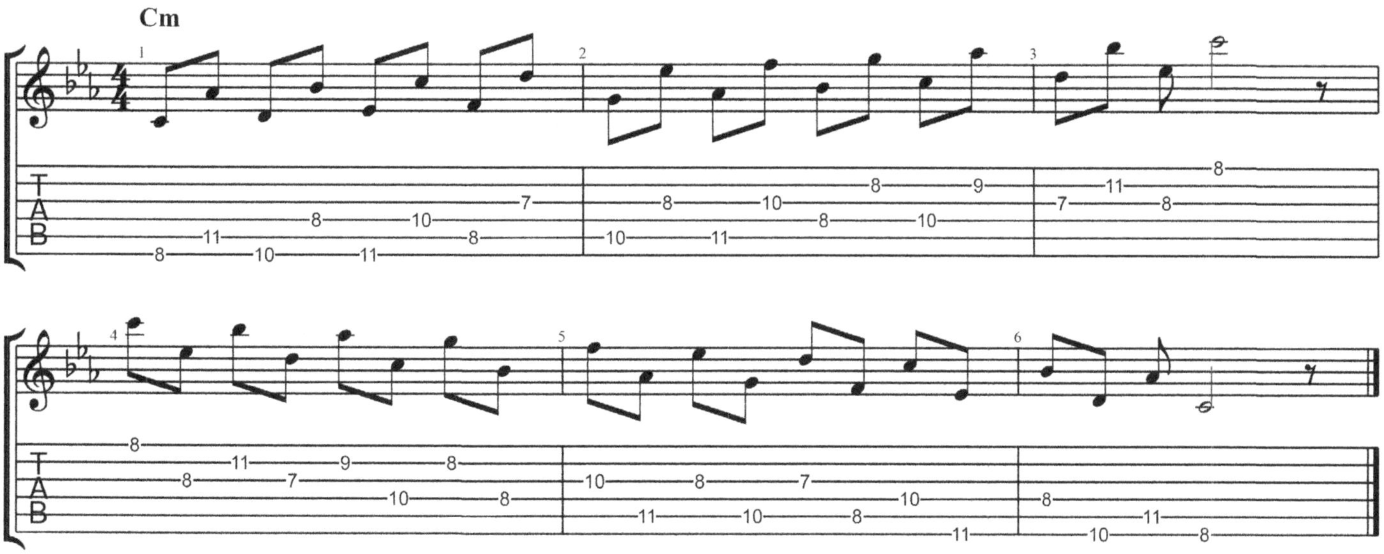

Now let's try out a few ideas using this scale.

I called this first lick *Corporate Ladder* because it climbs up the Aeolian scale. This one is derived from the notes of the C Minor Pentatonic scale and climbs up in 4th intervals.

Keep your hand close to eighth position throughout this lick. Like the previous stacked 4th licks, you'll need to bar your first finger across the bottom three strings at the 8th fret and play the Eb on the 11th fret, with your fourth finger.

I use the first finger to bar all the notes that fall on adjacent strings at the 8th fret, as it's the most economical fingering for the lick. Pay attention to the fingering on each descent, so you get the notes clean.

Example 2d – *Corporate Ladder*

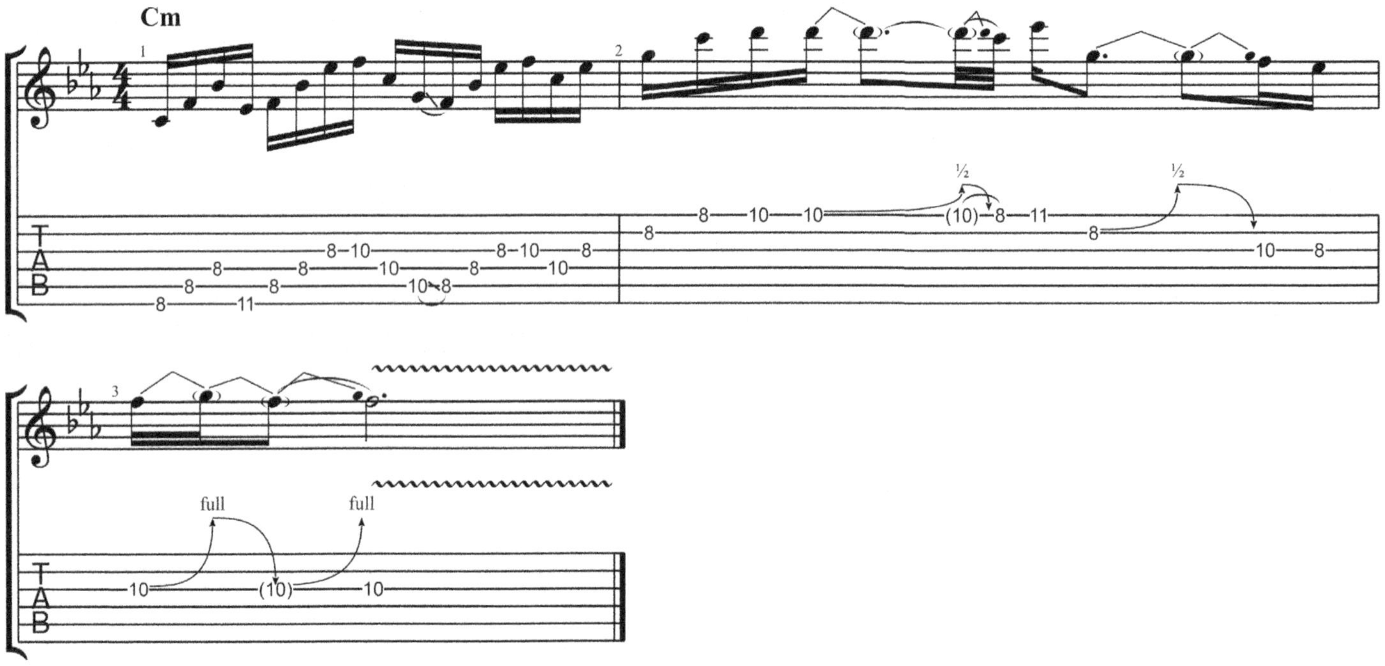

The next lick is based on 5th intervals. It's a snaking, sliding line that moves diagonally across the range of the neck. It works over a C minor or Cm7 chord.

Bar one is all about the rapid ascent up the fretboard. At the beginning of the lick, I avoid playing the root note and instead start with a four-note phrase that begins on the b7 of Cm7 (Bb). This, and the fact that I'm playing wide intervals, stops the lick from sounding predictable.

At the beginning of bar two there are two quick sweeps to execute. These patterns are a C minor triad and Bb Major triad respectively, each with one note of the triad doubled up.

The idea here is to use triads from other chords that belong to the same parent scale/key. At the beginning of the chapter we learned that the C Aeolian scale originates from the parent scale of Eb Major. C minor is chord vi in the key of Eb Major, and Bb7 (or Bb Major in triad form) is chord V.

Perform the sweeps by playing the high notes on the first string with the fourth finger, then jump to the first finger to begin each swept triplet phrase. Rake your pick upwards across the top three strings.

Example 2e – *Sliding into 5ths*

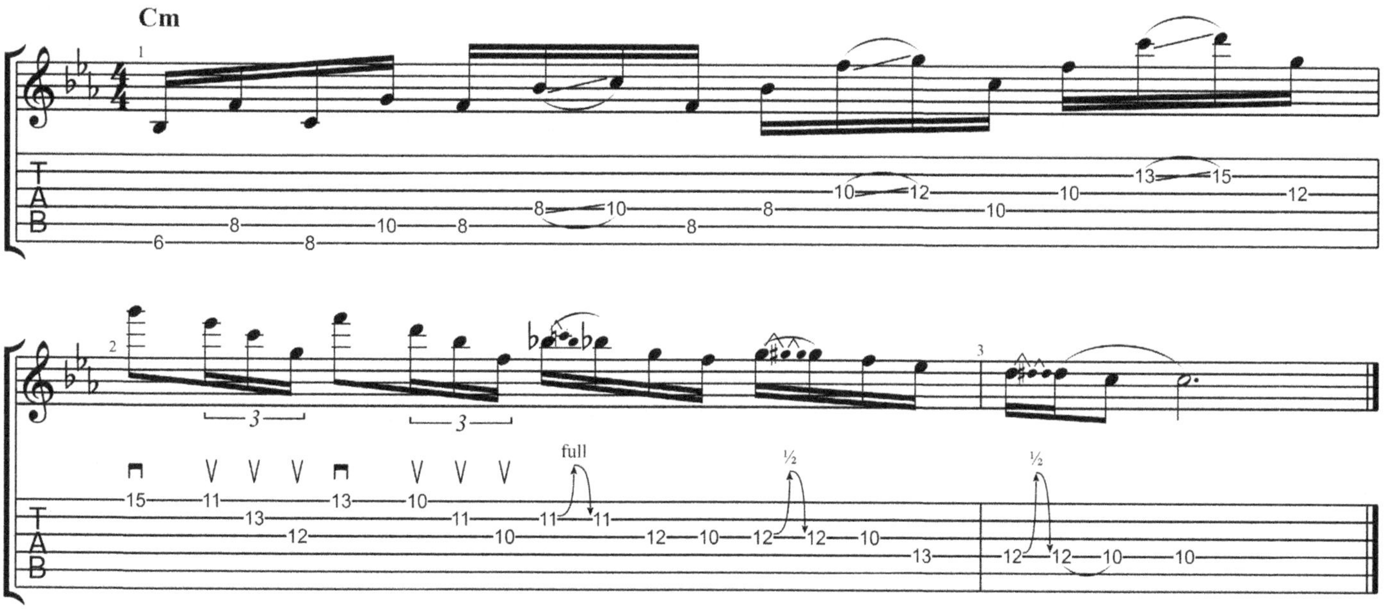

Here comes the 1–5–9 (root, 5th, 9th) shape again. It's one of my favorite shapes of all time! I love its ambiguous, spacious sound. Because there is no 3rd interval, this pattern can sound minor or major, depending on the musical context.

Bar one of this lick is fueled by ascending 1–5–9 movements which call for some quick fretting hand position changes. For each section, align the fretting hand ready, with fingers spread, a split second before you have to play the notes.

In bar two, keep your fretting hand in tenth position throughout to play the bluesy descending lick. The first four-note phrase here spells a G minor triad (another triad from the parent key of Eb Major. G minor is chord iii). The rest of the notes come from C Minor Pentatonic, punctuated with bends.

Example 2f – *159'er Breaker Breaker*

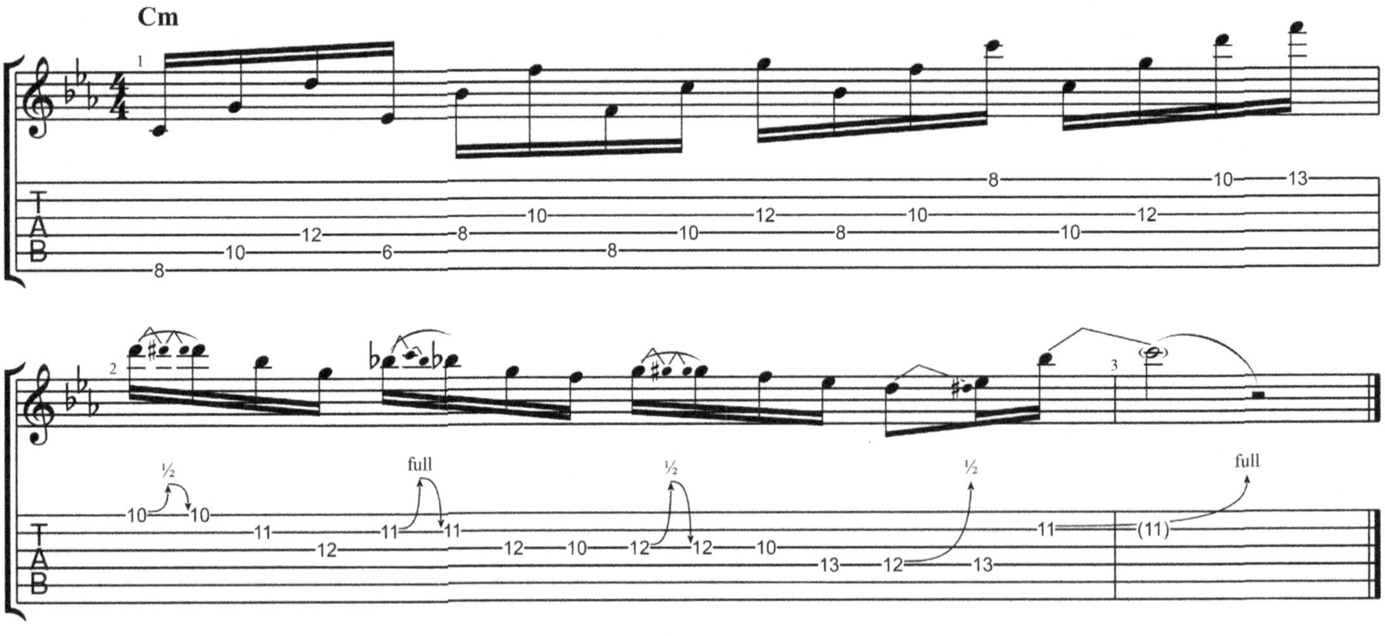

The first half of this next lick is a displaced blues scale. Play a standard C Minor Blues scale in eighth position, then work on just the first twelve notes of this lick to get a feel for the concept of displacement. The idea is that instead of playing the notes of the scale from bottom to top in the normal sequence, you *displace* certain notes an octave higher, then return to the original octave.

In bar two we have a brief scale pattern followed by a chromatic walk up the B string to an Eb (the b3 of the C minor chord). The lick ends with some standard Rock 'n' Roll bends.

Example 2g – *Dis Placemat*

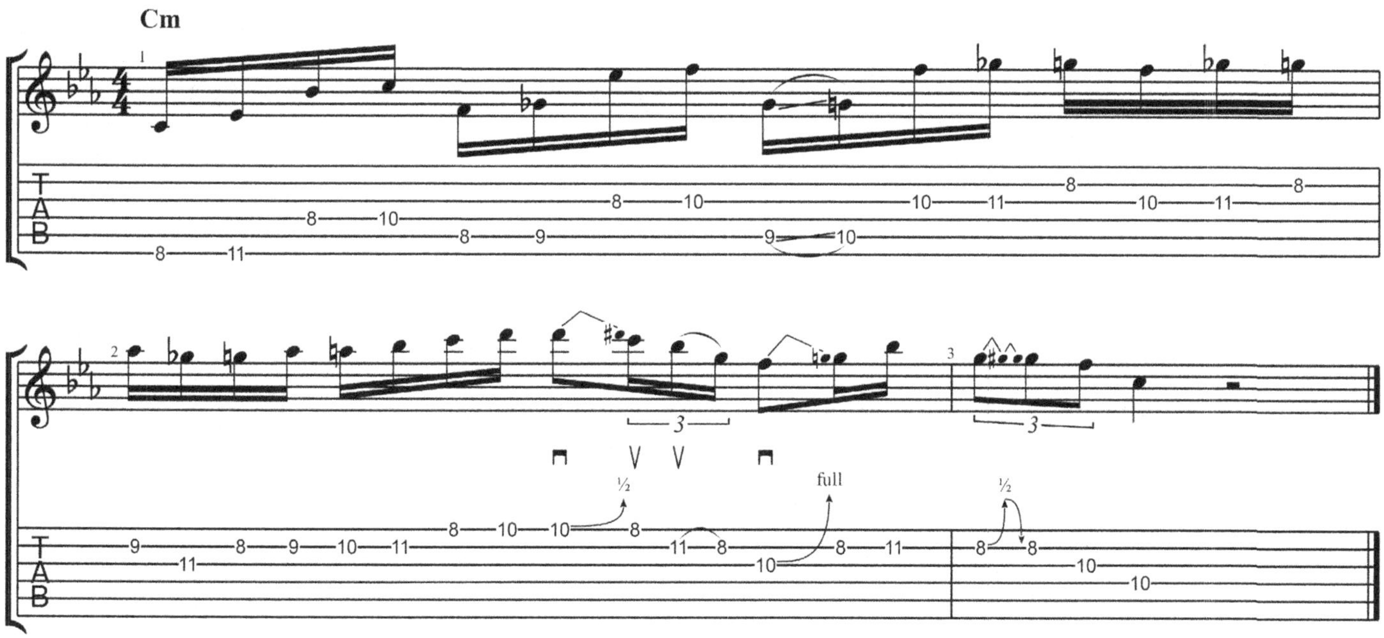

The final riff in our Aeolian segment begins on the "4&" of the pickup bar, a fraction before beat 1 of the first bar. The idea was to begin with some perfect 5th intervals and move into diatonic 6th jumps. Pay attention to your fingering and focus on playing the string skipping jumps super clean.

There are a couple of half-step index finger bends here before the last three whole step bends, and those final bends include a double-stop, adding in a high E string note.

Example 2h – *Andy One, Andy Two*

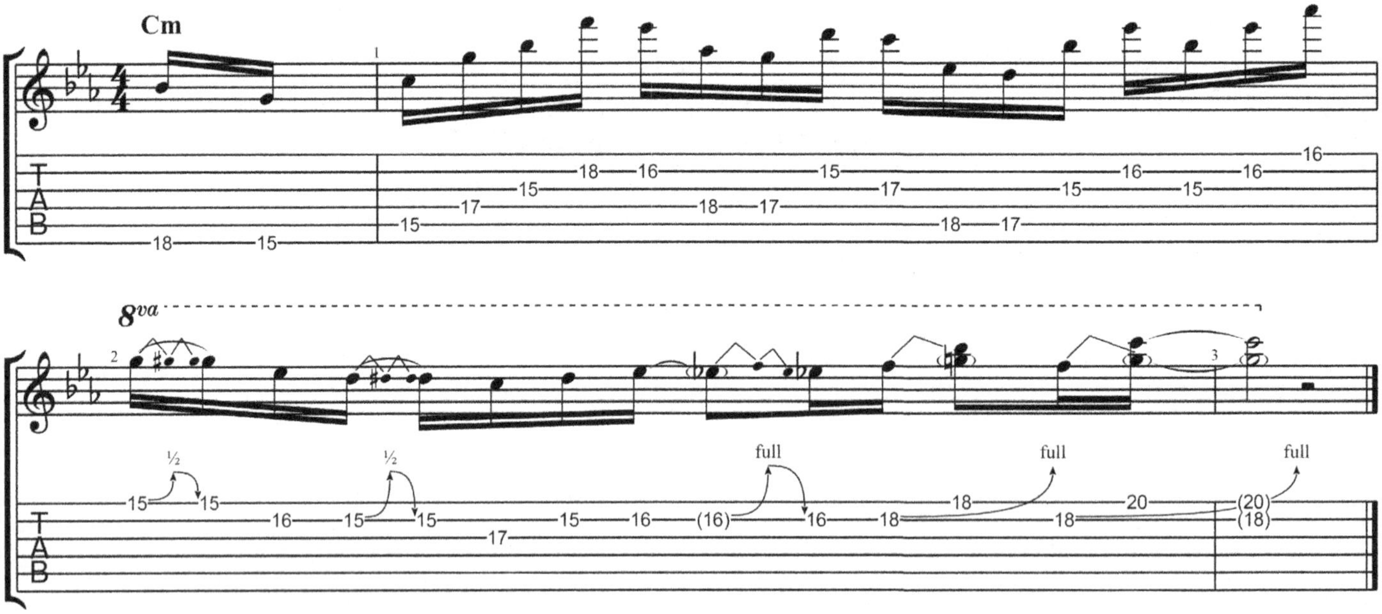

Chapter Three – Dorian Licks

About the Dorian Scale

In this chapter we'll focus on the other minor sound that's great to have under your fingers – the Dorian scale.

All the licks in this chapter are played over a D minor chord vamp using the D Dorian scale which is the second mode of its parent scale C Major. Dorian is identical to the Aeolian scale from its raised sixth degree which is responsible for giving it its unique color. It's a cool note when played over a minor chord because it creates a minor 6 sound – an idea often emphasized by Robben Ford.

D Dorian contains the notes: D, E, F, G, A, B, C.

Pink Floyd's famous *Another Brick in the Wall* was written in D Dorian. It's also the sound of Miles Davis' tune *So What* and Green Day's *Boulevard of Broken Dreams*.

The D Dorian scale contains all the notes of the D Minor Pentatonic scale within it (D, F, G, A, C), so that'll feature in some of the lines that follow.

Below is the A string root shape for D Dorian in fifth position. The available notes on the low E string are indicated by hollow circles, but you should learn the scale from its root note.

D Dorian

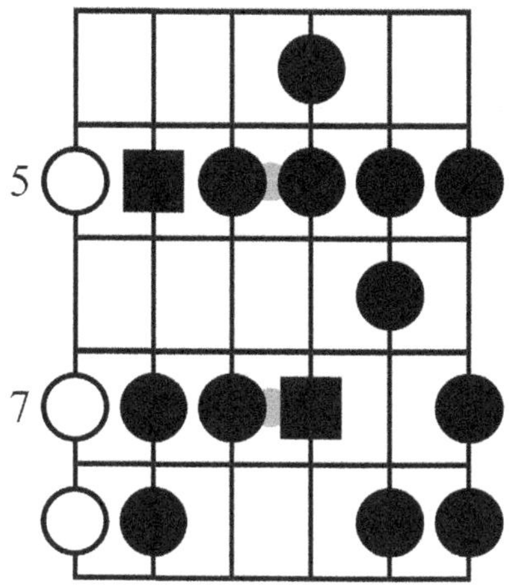

Here is the E string root shape for the scale in tenth position.

D Dorian

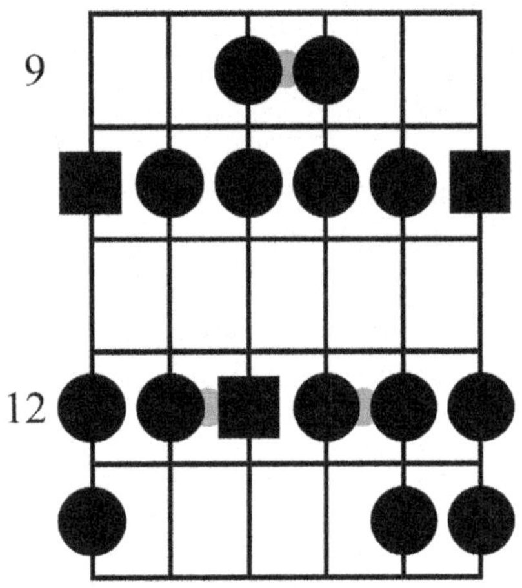

As before, let's drill a few Dorian interval exercises before getting into the licks. As with the Aeolian scale, we'll focus on 4ths, 5ths and 6ths. Occasionally, I'll break out of the scale's box shape if it makes the fingering for an interval much easier to manage.

We begin with 4ths, played using the A root position scale shape. I think you'll agree that the Dorian in 4ths is a pretty cool sound!

Example 3a

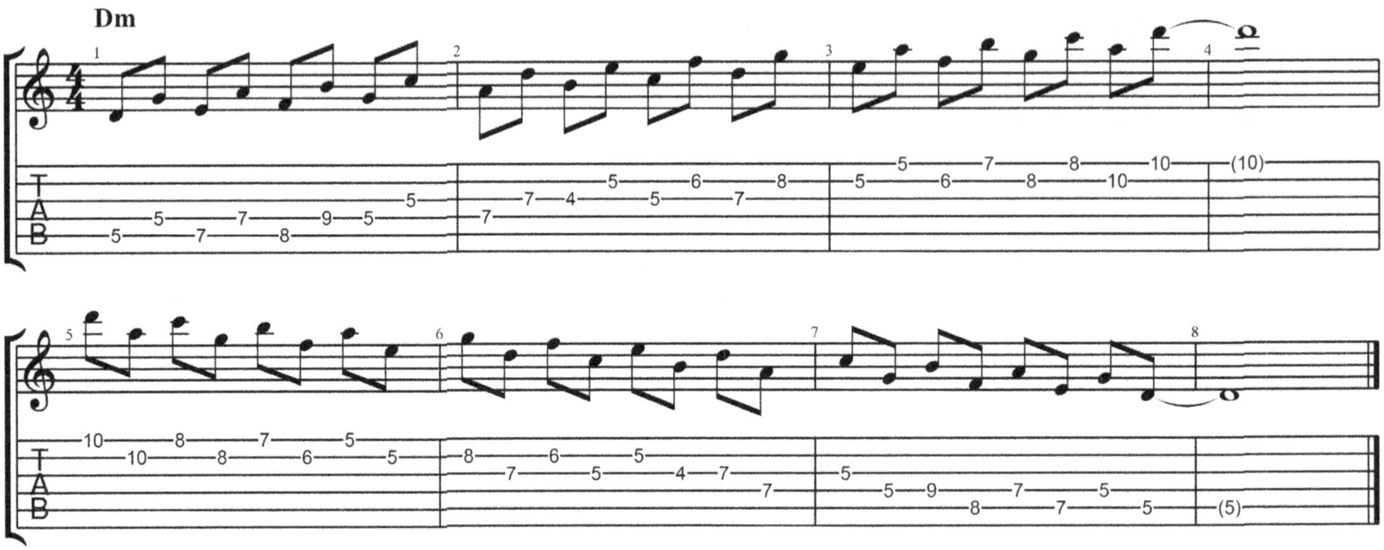

Now play through the scale using 5th intervals based around the higher E root position shape.

Example 3b

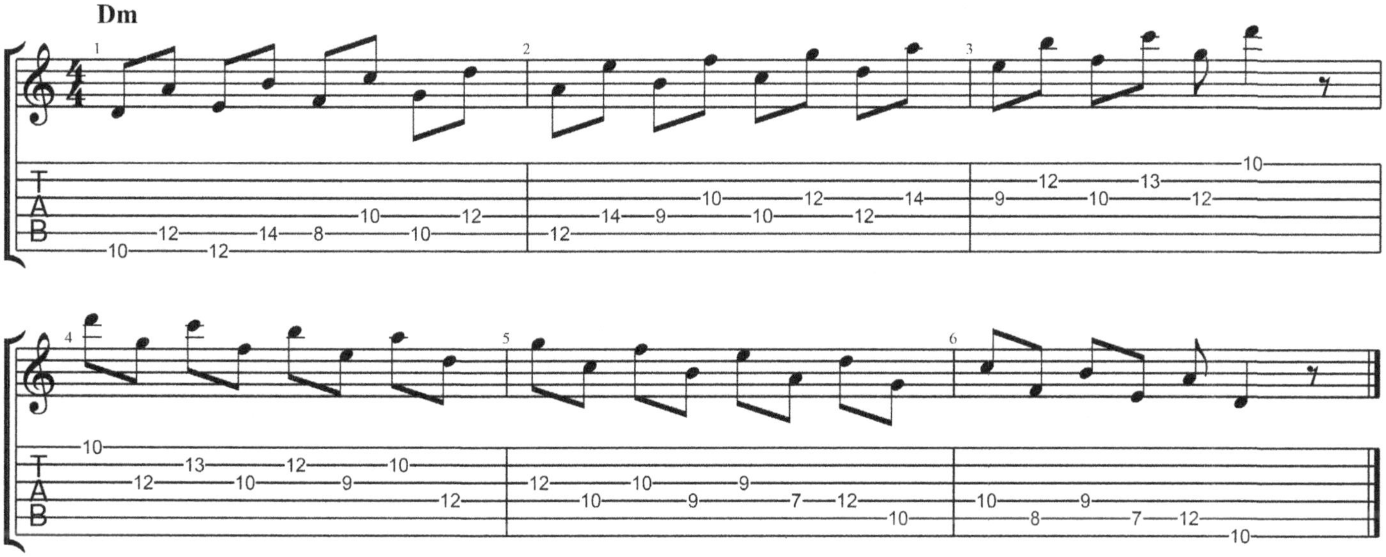

Finally, let's return to the fifth position shape to play the scale in 6ths.

Example 3c

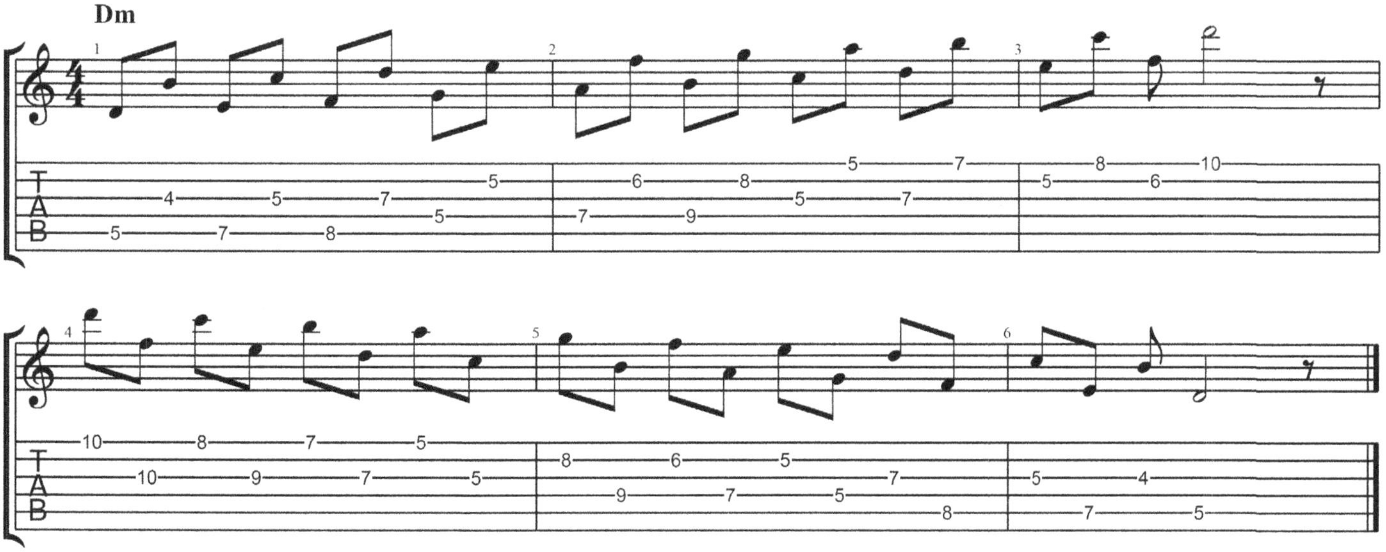

Now that you're familiar with some of the intervallic sounds of the Dorian scale, let's look at how these translate into some exciting licks.

We'll kick off with a lick I've called the *Blue Tude*. Not "tude" as in *etude*, but *attitude,* because this one is all about capturing an aggressive Rock 'n' Roll vibe.

This idea includes some sassy half step blues bends. It contains b5 as well as perfect 5th intervals, and also some slippery hammer-ons and pull-offs.

This is a longer lick than the ones you've encountered so far and spans four bars. Break it down into sections and perfect each part before joining it all together. You can also just grab any part of this line that you like and use it as a lick in its own right. Feel free to change it up and make it your own.

Bar one features a phrase that repeats across string sets with a little variation at the end. For the first two bends, I'm bending from the b5 interval to the 5th (G# to A), then from C# to D, approaching the root note from a half step below.

In bar two, the next group of sassy half step bends focus on movements from the 6th to the b7 (B to C) and the 9th to the b3 (E to F). You can hear the result of this approach is to create an outside-inside type of sound.

Bar three is the section of the lick that needs the most attention to play smoothly. In the first four-note phrase you'll hear the b5 interval again. The rest of that phrase, and the next four-note phrase, are arranged in perfect fifths.

The tricky part here is the sextuplet phrase that follows. I slide my first finger back and forth to execute this phrase. Work it out slowly to begin with, as it'll sound messy at speed if it's not played cleanly.

Example 3d – *Blue Tude*

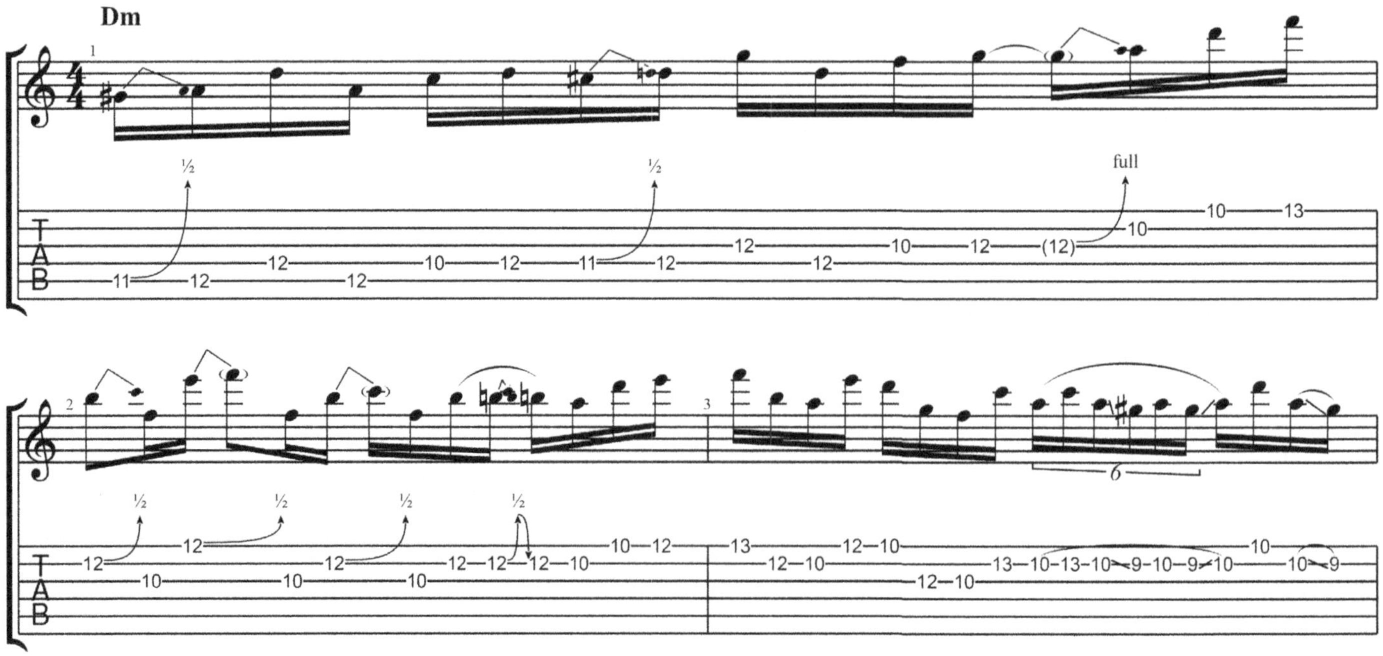

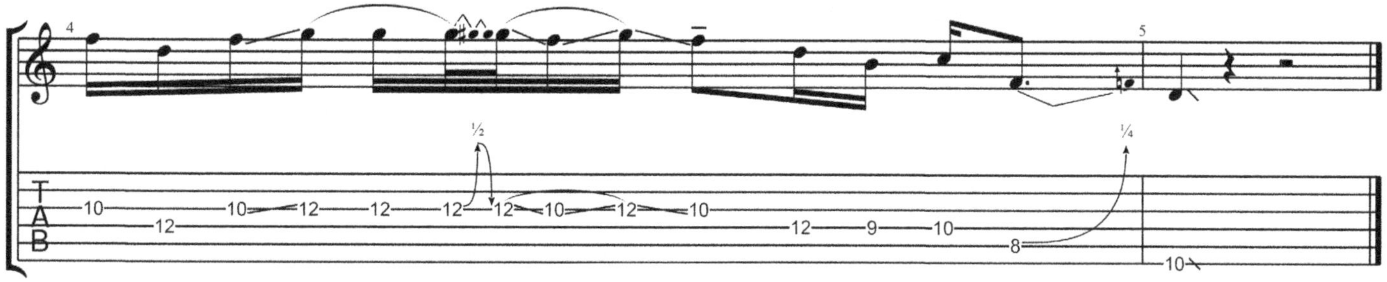

Next up is a line that ascends D Minor Pentatonic and descends with D Dorian. You should find the ascending hammer-on section in bar one pretty easy to play as there's not much picking required. If you want to achieve some speed in your runs, a combination of legato and picked phrases is a good place to start.

At the beginning of bar two I play a unison bend. Fret the D on the high E string with your first finger and execute the bend from 13th fret on the B string with the third finger while still sounding the D.

There are some 4ths in the descending pattern. In general, when playing perfect 4th intervals descending or ascending, I will bar the notes with one finger and roll that finger to keep them clearly separated. But if I have three or more notes descending on the same fret, I will often use separate fingers for cleaner execution.

Example 3e – *Hammer Time*

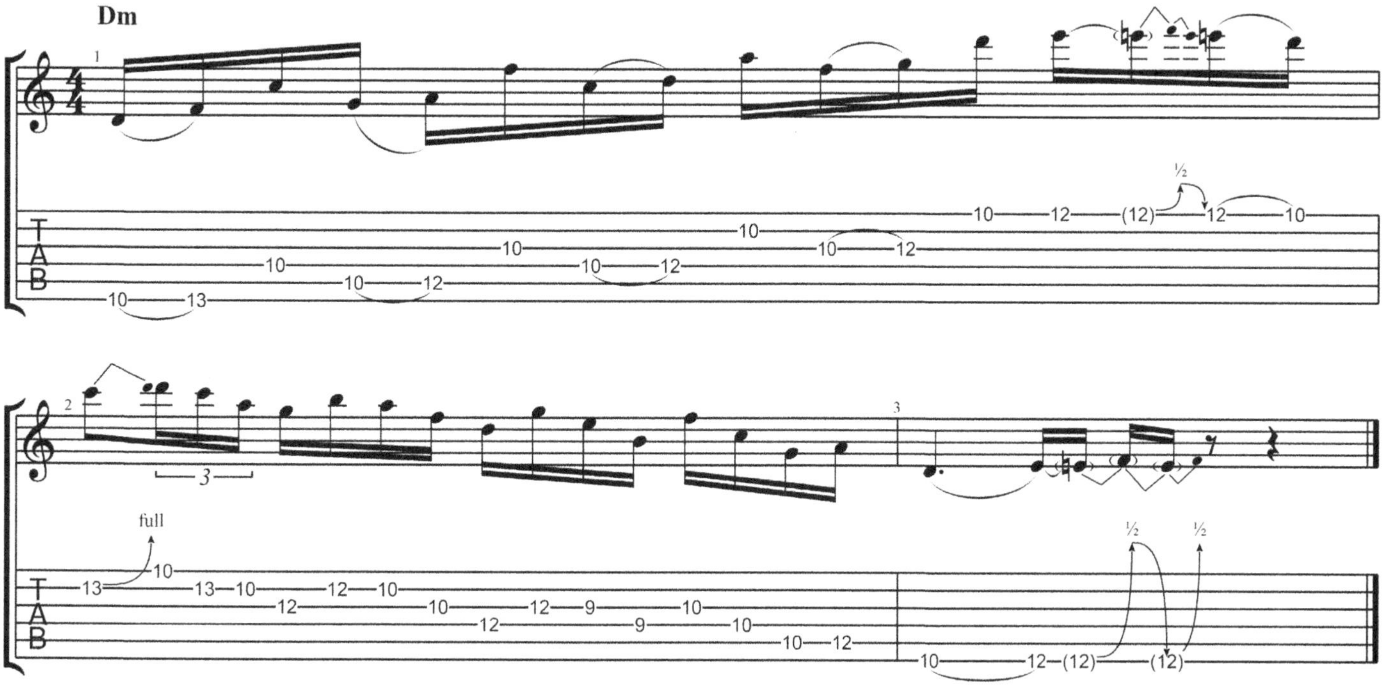

This line begins by using perfect 4ths ascending D Minor Pentatonic in the fifth position. Once again, the magic 4ths prove so useful in preventing the lick from sounding like a boring pentatonic cliché.

In bar two, the notes that are bent are the 6th (or 13th) scale degree to the b7 (and back), the b3 to the 4th, then the 9th to the b3, finally resolving to the root. I add a unison bend once the line has resolved.

This bending section is the highlight of the lick and needs to be played with tons of attitude, while you bend the heck out of those notes. Really wring every ounce of expression from this phrase!

Example 3f – *Bendy Booger*

I called this next lick *8va Sassy One*. In notation, 8va means "one octave higher" and the lick begins with some octave jumps. The notes come exclusively from D Minor Pentatonic while ascending and the line demands some fretting hand gymnastics to play it cleanly.

Here, I keep my fretting hand in tenth position throughout, and stick rigidly to the one-finger-per-fret rule. I finger the opening phrase as follows:

- First finger plays the D on the low E string
- Third finger plays the G at the 12th fret
- First finger moves behind it to play the F
- Fourth finger reaches over the top to play the low F octave note on the 13th fret low E string

Keeping to one finger per fret, you should be able to work out an economical fingering for the rest of bar one.

The rest of the lick is a bluesy line that ends by emphasizing the 6th degree of the scale, highlighting its Dorian personality.

Example 3g – *8va Sassy One*

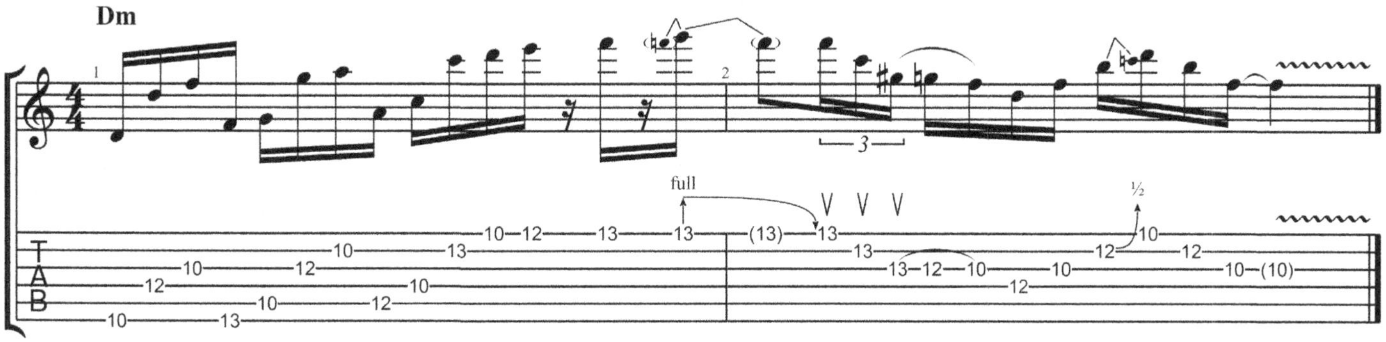

The final lick of this section is all about the string skipping. I love this technique because it's such an easy and direct way to open up your playing and avoid predictable runs that follow a linear sequence. Scale runs have their place, of course, but if you combine them with skipping ideas you can bring much greater contrast and interest into your playing and create some really cool lines.

Here, I climb the D Minor Pentatonic scale by skipping strings, then pick up one note from the string I skipped, before continuing the ascent.

On the descent, I add in some half step "attitude" bends prior to a 4ths descent on the 12th fret (which you'll need to play with separate fingers). The lick ends with three octaves of the root note.

Example 3h – *All Aboot Skippin'*

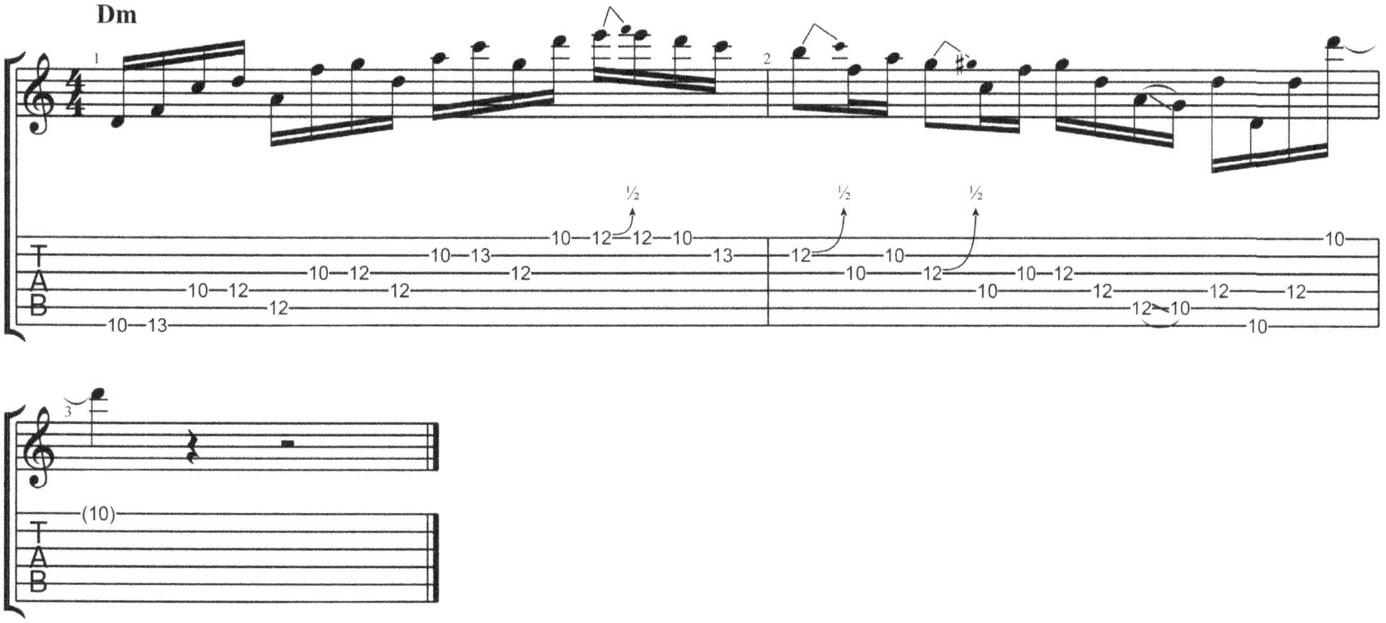

Chapter Four – Ionian / Major Licks

About the Ionian (Major Scale)

The Ionian mode is just another name for the plain old Major scale and so far, we've not explored any major licks so that'll be the focus of this chapter.

All the licks in this chapter are played over a D Major 7 chord vamp, and we'll use the D Ionian scale.

D Ionian contains the notes: D, E, F#, G, A, B, C#

Like the Dorian scale in the previous chapter, here are the A string, and E string root scale shapes for D Ionian.

First, the A string root shape in fifth position.

D Ionian (Major)

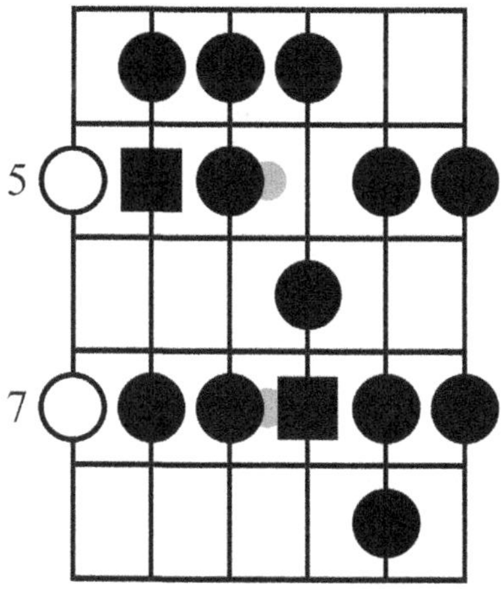

And now the E string root shape.

D Ionian (Major)

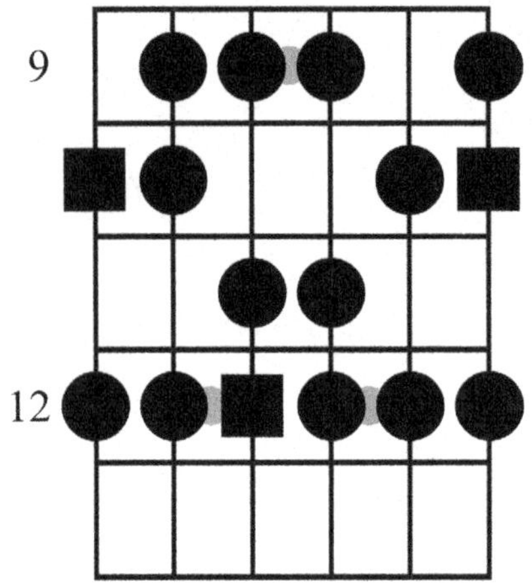

As familiar as you no doubt are with the major scale, you may not be used to breaking it down into intervals so here are the scale exercises in 4ths, 5ths and 6ths as before. I use all those intervallic jumps in the licks that follow. Here we go!

Here is D Ionian played in 4ths using the A string root shape. I extend the last few notes beyond the shape in order to finish on the root note.

Example 4a

Next, D Ionian ascending and descending in 5ths.

Example 4b

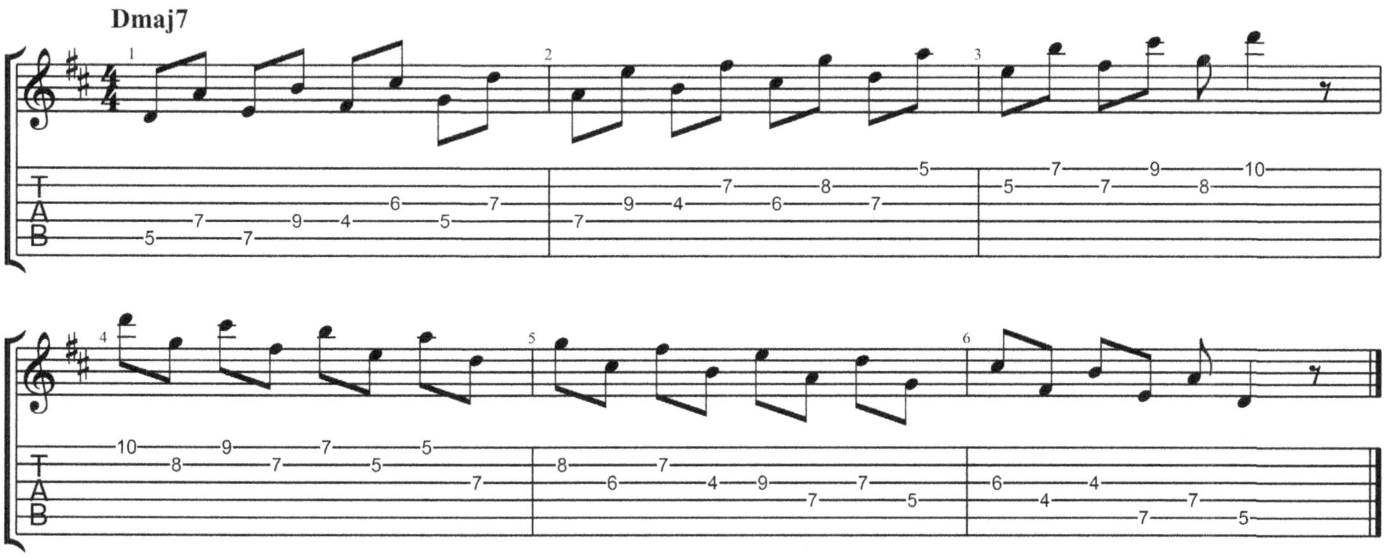

And finally, in 6ths – a more common use of the scale, but still worth drilling.

Example 4c

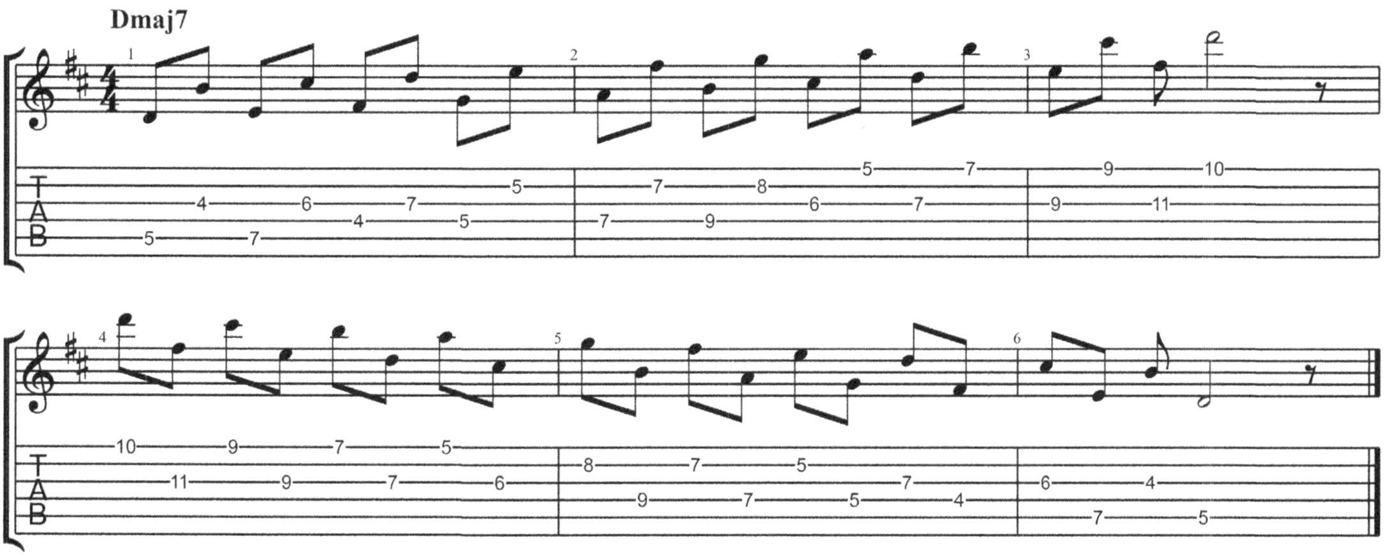

Now let's explore how we can change up this familiar scale with some intervallic licks.

In this first lick, my aim is to outline the sound of the DMaj7 chord by adding a couple of extended notes. In bar one, each cluster of four notes uses a different combination of D Ionian scale tones, which emphasize different DMaj7 colors.

The first four notes spell out the safe combination of root, 5th, root and 3rd.

The next group of notes highlights the more colorful 6th (B), 9th (E), 5th and root, and so on.

In bars 2-3 I work the D Ionian scale notes in one small zone of the neck and keep things interesting by adding bluesy bends. On the B string, the notes are bent from a B (6th) to C# (7th).

In the final bar, the half step bend from F# to G creates a cool effect. F# is the 3rd of the DMaj7 chord and superimposing the G on top implies the sound of Dmaj11.

Example 4d – *Outlinin'*

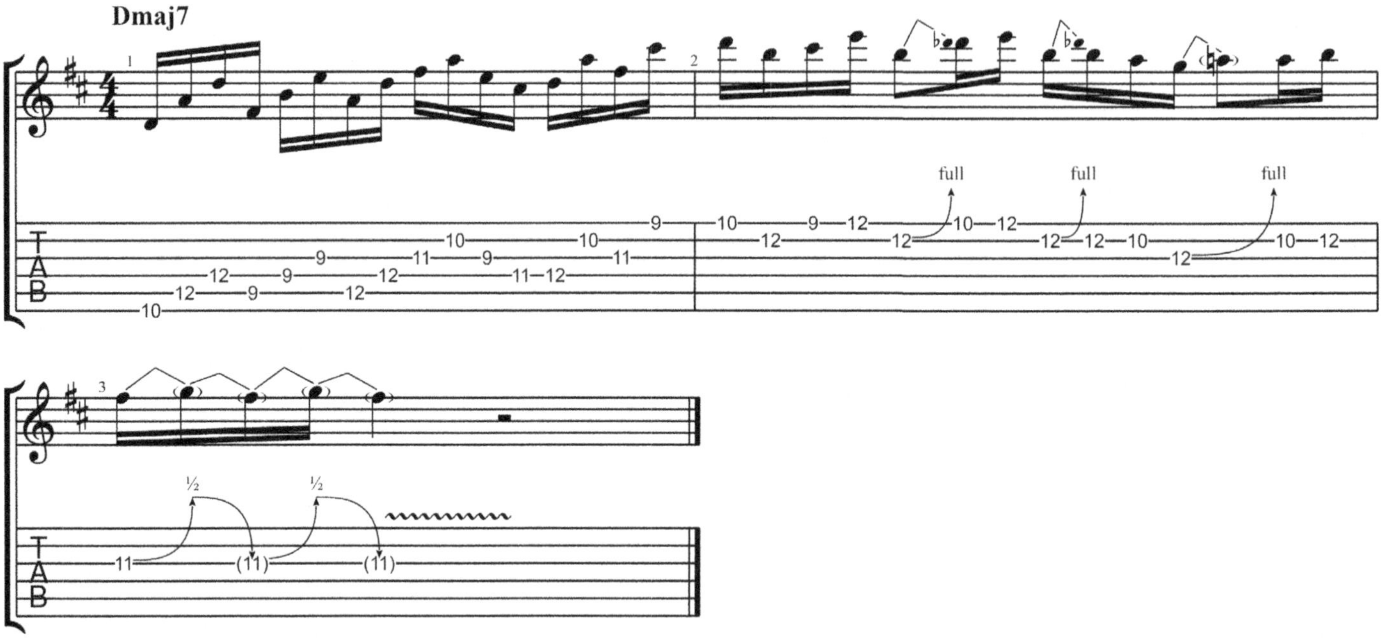

No prizes for guessing why I called this next lick *Four!* It's centered around diatonic 4th intervals and highlights the cool, spacious sounds that are locked away inside the major scale when we dig into it a bit deeper.

You may have noticed in the scale exercises at the beginning of the chapter that not every 4th interval is a *perfect 4th*. It's tempting to think that when we talk about "4ths" they are always located on the same fret on the adjacent string, but of course it depends entirely on how the degrees of the scale are arranged.

This is why using scale exercises that drill just one interval are so important – it's good to recognize the patterns on the fretboard, as well as having the *sound* of a 4th interval locked in your head.

I view the first part of the lick as two groups of 1/8th notes, each beginning with a similar sequence. When you're soloing with larger intervals, using sequences and patterns makes it easier for the audience to grasp what's going on.

The lick ends in bar two with a series of bends. That final wide bend moves from an F# (3rd of DMaj7) to A (5th) and back again. It's a cool sound over DMaj7.

Example 4e – *Four!*

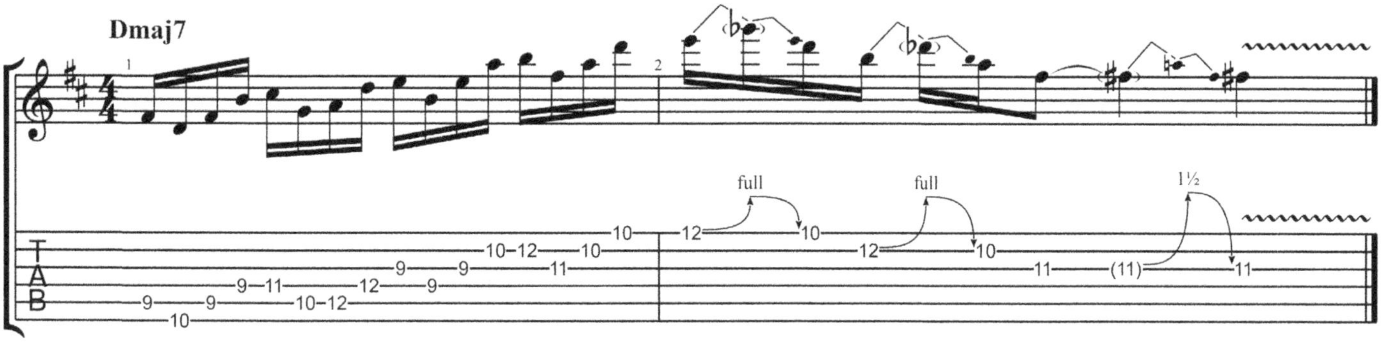

By now, you should be getting more comfortable with playing in 5ths and the next idea begins with a stack of them. Notice that 5ths provide an easy way to ascend the neck quickly into the upper register.

I called this lick *5th Question* because often it's tempting to resolve licks predictably and always return to the root note. Instead, take a bigger view of your solo. A solo is like telling a story and you eventually realize that you don't have to resolve every line. A lick can end on a question (like this one, which ends on the 3rd of DMaj7) before the *following lick* gives an answer.

Keep your fretting hand in ninth position throughout this lick and everything will be within easy reach. At the end of the lick, make sure you get the final bend up to pitch and hold it there for a split second before applying the wide vibrato.

Example 4f – *5th Question*

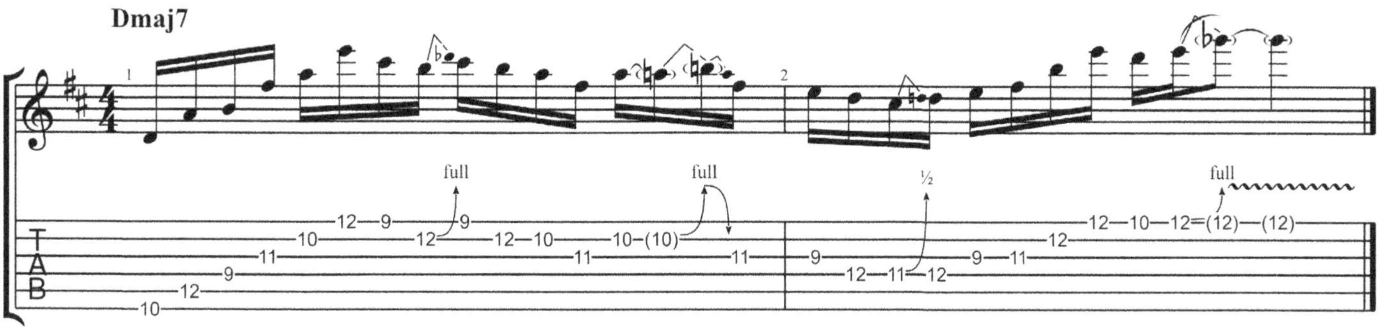

Next is a melodic sounding D Ionian lick that begins with some half step hammer-on and pull-off movements and includes some perfect 5ths and ends with a few Rock 'n' Roll bends.

Bar one contains a question-and-answer phrase. The rhythm and string skipping idea of the opening six-note phrase is immediately repeated on a different string set. In the first phrase, after the hammered notes, the melody skips up to the root note on the 10th fret.

In the answering phrase the target note is the E on the third string, 9th fret. You might notice that the hammered notes in this phrase move from the 5th (A) to the b5 (Ab) and back. Ab doesn't belong to the D Ionian mode, but it's played so fleetingly that it doesn't cause any real tension. It's more like a bebop style approach note, and the fact that it's played on an upbeat also helps it blend in!

In bar two, after the ascending 5ths, the ending consists of a simple melody with a couple of whole step bends, ending on the 5th.

Example 4g – *Half Baked*

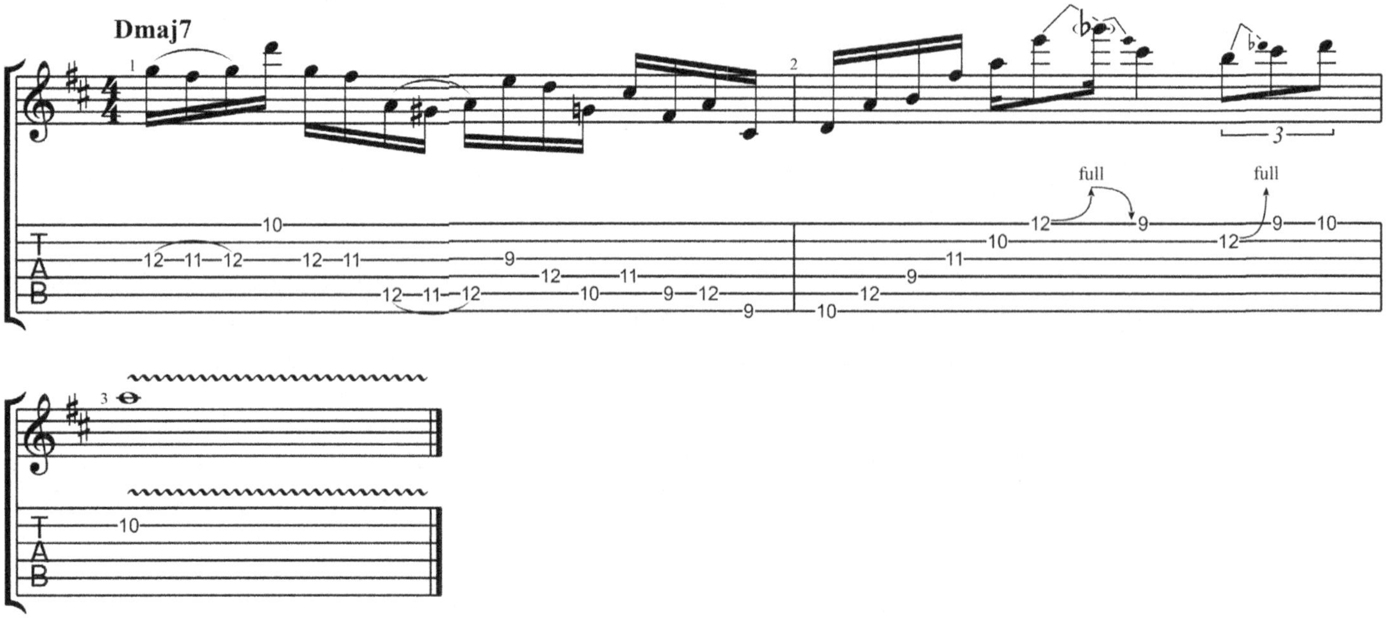

This next lick jumps strings from the A to the G to the high E which means an unusual stretch that spans five frets from the 5th to the 9th.

If that feels like too much for you, after the D on the A string, 5th fret, shift your fretting hand position forward slightly before playing the F# on the 9th fret with your fourth finger.

This lick is fueled mostly by 3rds and 6ths.

Example 4h – *Jumpy Dude*

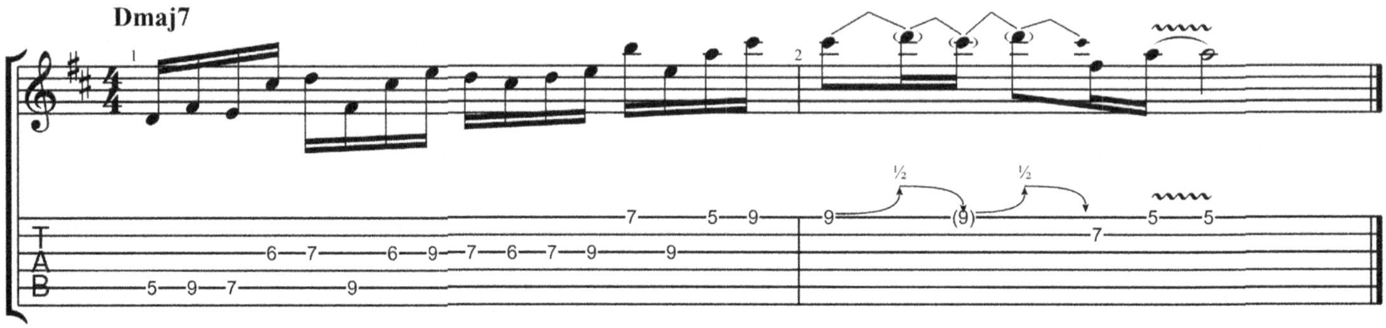

The next example is based on 6ths and will work well over a D6, DMaj9 or DMaj7 chord.

Your fretting hand should look a bit spidery if you're playing this line in the most economical way. Keep your fretting hand hovering around seventh position and stretch out your fourth finger to reach the notes on the 10th fret.

The idea is to play a sequence of six scale notes that repeats twice. Using groups of six notes, rather than the expected four or eight, adds rhythmic interest and gives the lick a kind of forward motion.

Example 4i – *Sixy Spider Sequel*

As well as playing whole passages using a single type of interval, you can of course mix things up and combine them in smaller groups, like I do here. This lick begins by combining intervals starting with a perfect 5th, followed by a 4th, then back to a 5th.

As the ascending phrase finishes, it is followed by a DMaj7 arpeggio. Although the notes are played out of sequence, you'll find this phrase easier to play if you visualize a DMaj7 chord shape on the top four strings, with your first finger on the high E string, 9th fret. Assign the appropriate finger to each note as if you were playing that chord, ending with your fourth finger on the D at the 12th fret.

For the F# that follows, hop your first finger over to play it, and the rest of the lick should fall logically under your fingers.

With any phrase, it's important to anticipate fingerings a note or two in advance, to avoid getting into a bind.

Example 4j – *5 Fo'5*

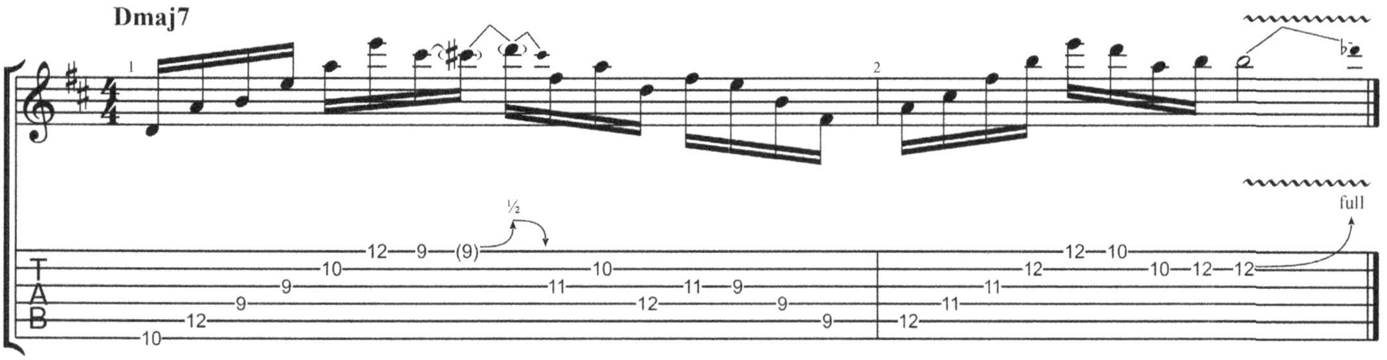

Here's the final D Ionian lick of this chapter. I named it *Ann Drogyny* because it can work over two different chords.

The idea comes from the D Major Pentatonic scale, but there's no 7th, and it could therefore happily be played over a D7 or DMaj7 chord.

It begins by climbing the scale in 4ths. Keep your first finger in third position throughout to finger this one.

Example 4k – *Ann Drogyny*

Chapter Five – Diminished Licks

About the Diminished Scale

The Diminished Scale has been used to great effect in modern rock guitar playing, so I wanted to include a chapter featuring some of my diminished lick ideas for you to try out.

The Diminished is a *symmetrical* scale, which means that it is built from a repeating pattern of intervals. In this case, the Diminished scale is built from alternating half steps and whole steps. You can begin the scale by playing a whole step or a half step, but the latter is the more commonly used version among guitar players and is known as the Half-Whole Diminished. It contains the following intervals:

Root, b9, #9, 3, #11, 5, 13, b7

You can tell just by looking at these intervals that the scale contains some pretty tense, dark sounding notes. All the licks that follow are played over an A Diminished chord, so we'll use the A Diminished scale.

A Half-Whole Diminished contains the notes: A, Bb, C, C#, D#, E, F#, G

Here are the box position shapes for this scale with root notes on the low E and A strings.

First, the fifth position E string root shape.

A Half-Whole Diminished

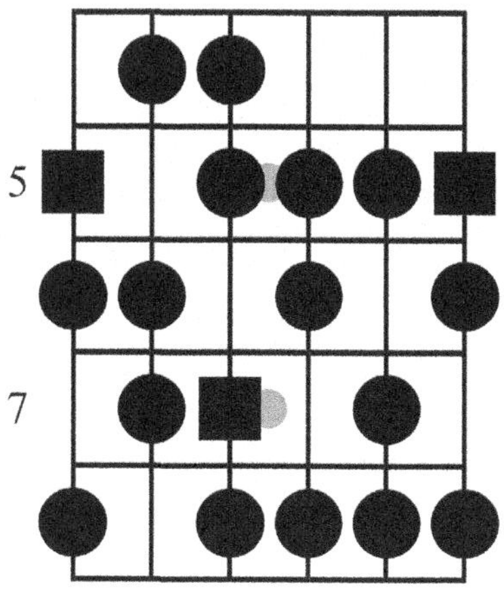

And here is the A string root shape.

A Half-Whole Diminished

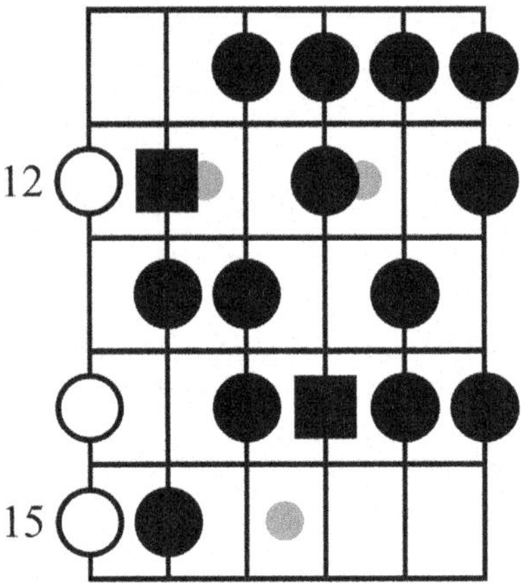

As always, I've indicated the available scale tones on the low E string with hollow circles, but it's best to learn these patterns from the root note to train your ears to recognize how each scale interval relates to the root note.

Because of the symmetrical nature of this scale, it's also worth practicing the climbing pattern below.

This scale is easy to memorize because it has the exact same pattern of notes on each string, and it's also useful for playing diminished runs that quickly ascend the neck. I included the high A on the top string for completeness.

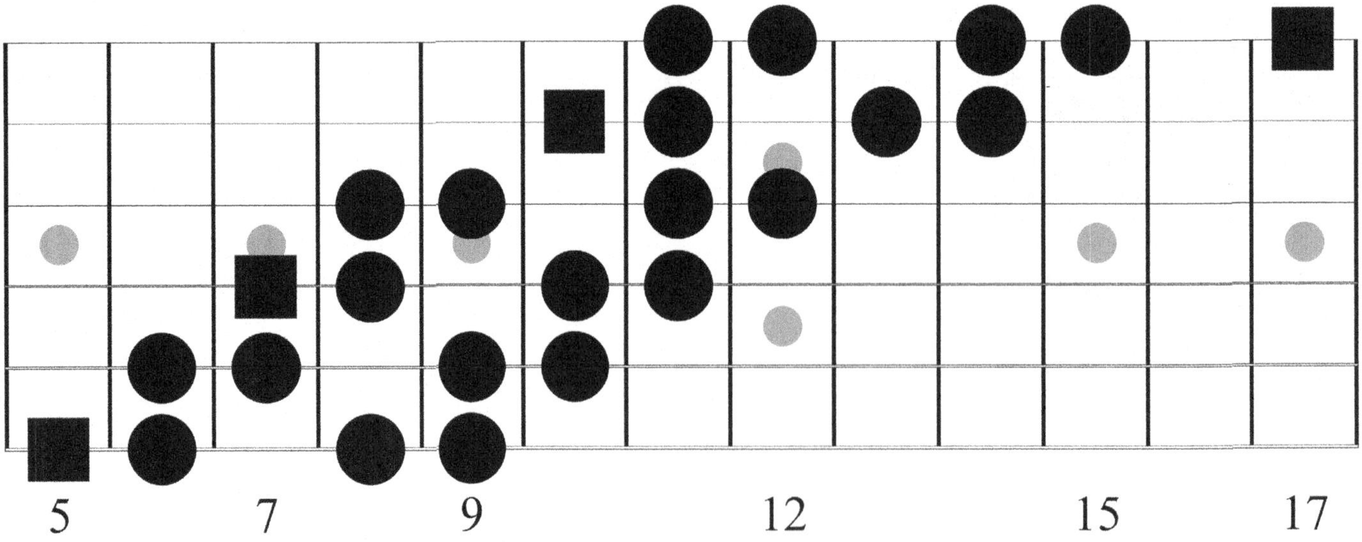

You can play this pattern most efficiently using a position slide. Play the first note on each string with the first finger, then immediately slide up one fret to play the second note also with the first finger.

Fret the remaining notes as you would normally.

Execute the index finger slide on *every* string. Practice this small economical movement and you'll soon be ascending the pattern rapidly.

To descend the pattern, play the highest note on each string with the fourth finger, the next note with the third finger, the next with the first finger, then slide down one fret to play the final note of the pattern also with the first finger.

Before we get into the licks, let's drill the A Diminished scale with a few interval exercises. This time we're going to play through it in 3rds, 4ths and 6ths.

First, play through the scale in 3rds. Normally, playing in 3rds creates quite a stable sound, but when we apply them to the evil sounding Diminished scale, you'll notice that it sounds as though it never really resolves.

Example 5a

Now let's try it with 4ths.

Due to the unusual construction of the diminished scale, it's not as easy to predict where the 4ths will fall on the fretboard. That's why exercises like this one are important – there's no substitute for drilling the scale and internalizing the *sound* of its intervals, so that your ears can tell you if you're playing it right.

Example 5b

Now play through the scale in 6ths.

Example 5c

You can get as creative as you like with this scale when practicing and it worth creating repeating patterns to practice that'll further embed its character in your ears.

Here's an exercise that uses the scale shape with its root on the A string beginning with the D# note on the first string, 11th fret before descending downward. Each note in the scale pattern is played twice as a kind of pedal tone. In bar seven, the pattern breaks as we reach the A root note and instead the exercise has a resolving ending.

Experiment with the scale and see if you can create your own similar patterns.

Example 5d

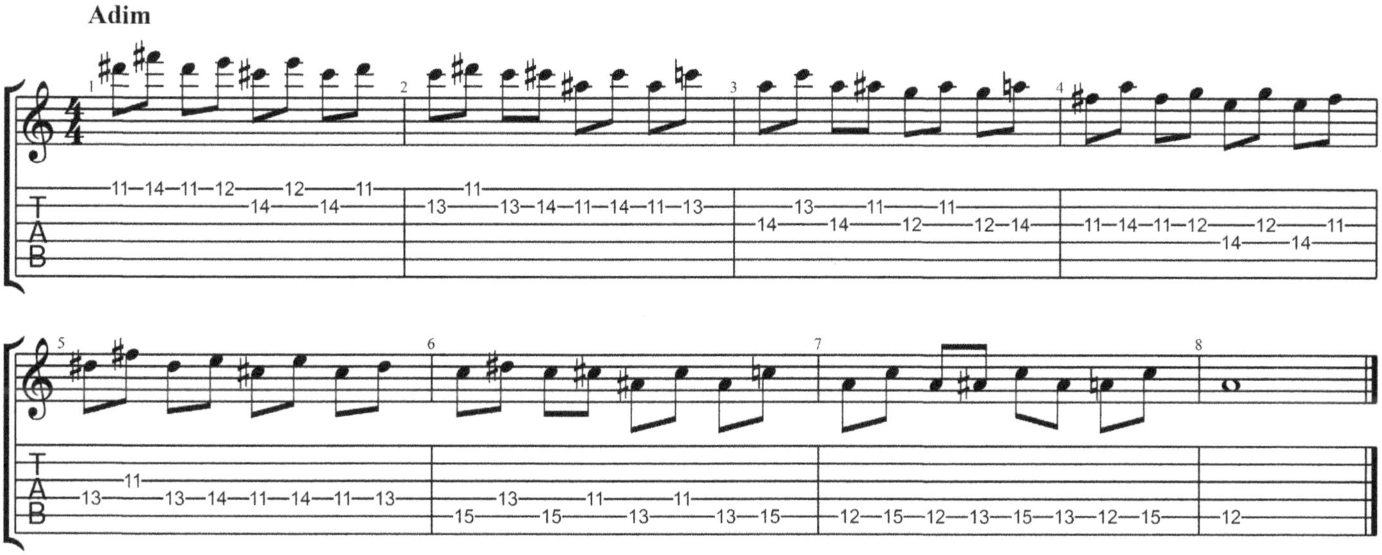

Now let's see how we can incorporate Diminished ideas into some cool licks.

One of the great things about the Diminished scale's symmetrical layout is the fact that the pattern repeats across the fretboard in minor thirds (every four frets).

This means the A Diminished scale contains the same notes as the C Diminished scale (C is a minor third above A), the Eb Diminished scale, and the Gb Diminished scale!

They all contain the same notes, they just have different starting points.

This means two things for us:

1. We can play the A Diminished licks below over four different diminished chords (A, C, D# and F#) and they will work.

2. We can create Diminished licks by playing a phrase and moving it around the fretboard in minor thirds.

In this first lick, I play the scale in 6ths as it gradually slides up the fretboard on two separate strings.

The line ends with a minor third bend. (You can always bend any note of this scale up a minor third).

Example 5e – *Slippery Slope*

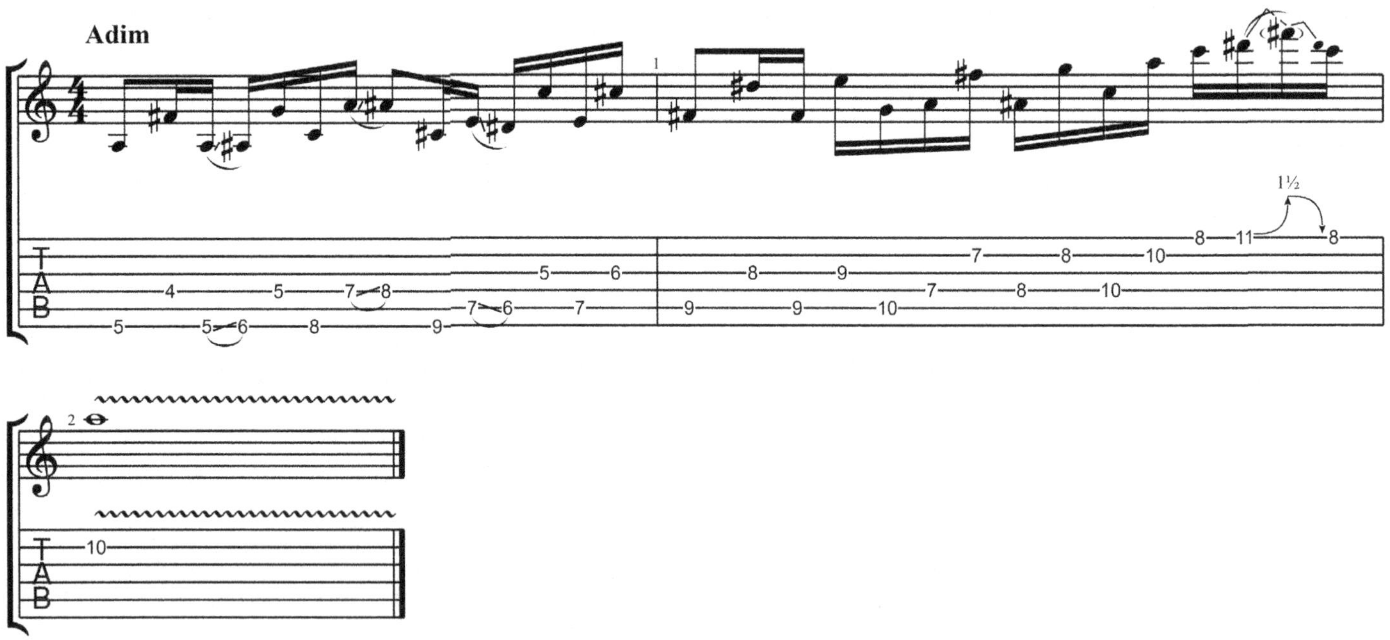

All diminished licks sound tense – hat's their job! We've already learned that one diminished lick can work successfully over four different diminished chords, but I also want to drop in the thought here that diminished licks will also work over dominant 7 chords.

The backing track for this chapter is an A diminished chord vamp, but for future reference you can practice these licks over an A7 chord too.

OK, so why does that work?

Let's remind ourselves of the scale tones.

A Half-Whole Diminished contains the notes: A, Bb, C, C#, D#, E, F#, G

An A7 chord is constructed A (root), C# (3rd), E (5th), G (b7)

Notice that every chord tone is contained within the scale. Played over an A7 chord, the other notes of the scale become extended or altered notes, as indicated in the table below.

A	Bb	C	**C#**	D#	**E**	F#	**G**
Root	b9	#9	3rd	b5 or #11	5th	13	b7

But guess what? The rabbit hole goes even deeper.

Just as our A Diminished licks will work over four diminished chords, they'll also work over four dominant chords.

You can also move the A7 chord in minor thirds (A7, C7, D#7, F#7). All the notes of those four dominant chords are contained within the A Diminished scale.

OK, this is not a book on diminished scale soloing, but suffice to say, there is a lot you can do with this scale! If you want to create either a pure diminished or an altered dominant sound, it's the ultimate scale for being able to recycle licks. Explore some of these ideas in your practice times.

Now, here's another diminished line that moves diagonally up the fretboard. On each string, I fret the first note with my first finger, then slide it into the second note.

Beware of how the pattern physically changes when played across the G and B strings, before it returns to normal on the top two strings. The lick ends with another minor third bend.

Example 5f – *Weirdo*

For the next line I climb an A# Diminished 7 arpeggio and playing the arpeggio notes out of sequence means that it ascends in b5 intervals.

At the beginning of bar two, we have a slightly unconventional "adapted" blues lick on the high E string. Here, the D at the 10th fret is bent up a half step to D#, but then released and the D# note is actually played before moving to C.

Normally, it would be natural to release the bend and play D to C, but the D is not in the arpeggio/scale, so we have to adapt this standard bluesy lick to accommodate the diminished scale.

I play a similar unison bend on the B string, moving from G# to A, but the G# isn't really heard, as it's the note A I want to emphasize.

I do the same thing again on the G string, bending the F at the 10th fret to an F#. The F doesn't belong to the A Diminished scale either, and here it's just being used for effect – to go from an outside to an inside sound.

Example 5g – *Flat 5th of Jack*

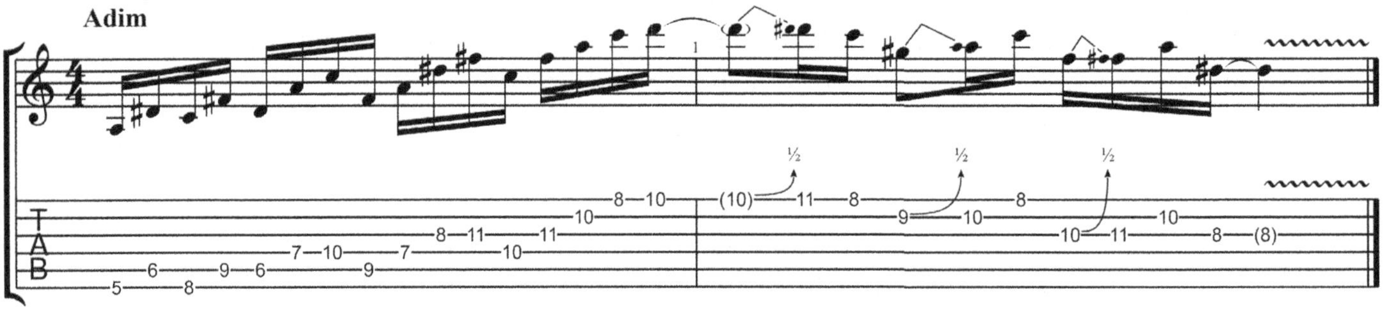

I call the following two-handed tapping diminished arpeggio lick *Dudley Do-Right.*

If you've never seen this classic cartoon, look it up on YouTube. Every time the heroine gets tied to the railroad tracks you hear a diminished sound!

Let me break this one down for you. It opens with an eight-note phrase. The first four notes spell out the diminished arpeggio.

The first two notes (5th and 8th frets) are tapped with the fretting hand (first finger, then fourth finger).

The second two notes (11th and 14th frets) are tapped with the picking hand (first finger, then fourth finger).

Then, the next four notes are just a repetition of the last two notes of the arpeggio, played on different strings.

Next I hop over onto the A string, where I play the four-note diminished arpeggio, but then begin again with the pattern I just described. This doubling up of arpeggio notes helps to keep the line flowing forward and gives it momentum.

One tip I'll pass on here is that I always keep my thumb resting on the top of the neck when tapping a line like this. It creates stability in the fretting hand and is much better than just hovering your hand over the fretboard. The thumb also acts as a guide as you slide up and down the neck. This way, you can tap accurately and cleanly every time.

If you're interested in developing your tapping technique further, you might also want to consider getting hold of a string dampener to keep the open strings quiet. You can get the one that I use direct from my web store at **www.jenniferbatten.com/product/string-dampers/**

Example 5h – *Dudley Do-Right*

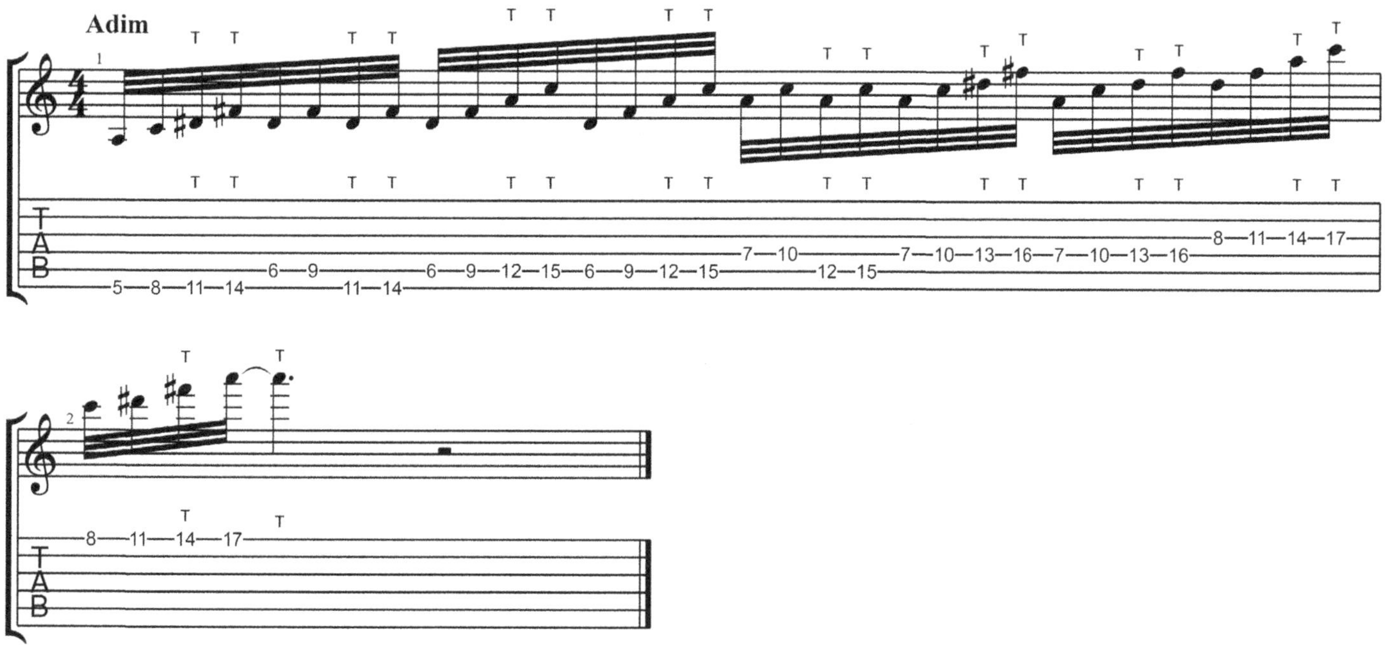

The next line is based on major 6th intervals. In bar one, from the root note of I play a major 6th above, then slide up a half step, then play a major 6th below. Then I jump up a perfect 4th onto the next string to repeat the pattern. During the third sequence, the pattern is broken and resolved.

The fingering is important here. The first two four-note phrases are played with the first and second fingers. When you play the third four-note grouping, play the first note with the second finger, and the next with the third finger.

This will prepare the fretting hand for what's next. Slide up a half step, then roll over onto the first string to play the C at 8th fret. After this note is played, the first finger jumps back onto the B string to execute the half step bend at the 7th fret.

Example 5i – *Steady Climber*

The following idea includes some monstrous minor 3rd bends that lead into diminished arpeggio sweeps.

The bends are played fast, so be sure to be accurate and get the full extent of the bend. After the opening bend, the arpeggio is played by raking upwards across the strings. This idea is repeated on the adjacent string.

The lick ends with diminished scale steps. You can apply plenty of vibrato to these as the lick finishes and play the whole thing with lots of attitude.

Example 5j – *Big Bad Bend*

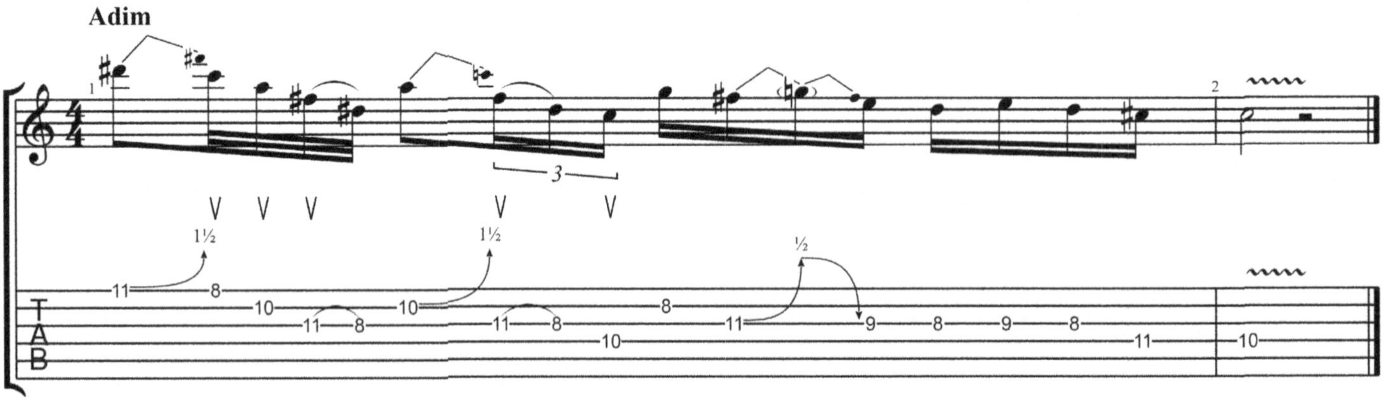

Chapter Six – Minor Pentatonic Licks

About the Pentatonic Scale

The minor pentatonic is the scale most guitar players learn when they first start playing. In fact, some players are still stuck there years later! But the pentatonic scale has a lot more to offer than the clichéd blues licks everyone knows. We can also use it to create some cool intervallic licks and spice things up, so that it doesn't sound routine.

In this chapter we'll be playing over an A minor vamp and using the A Minor Pentatonic scale.

A Minor Pentatonic contains the notes: A, C, D, E, G

It's best to learn this scale as five distinct shapes to begin with – which is easier to do compared to other scales, as it only has five notes. The aim is to work with the shapes so that you can eventually transition from one to the next seamlessly, covering the whole range of the fretboard.

For your reference, here are the five shapes:

A Minor Pentatonic
Shape 1

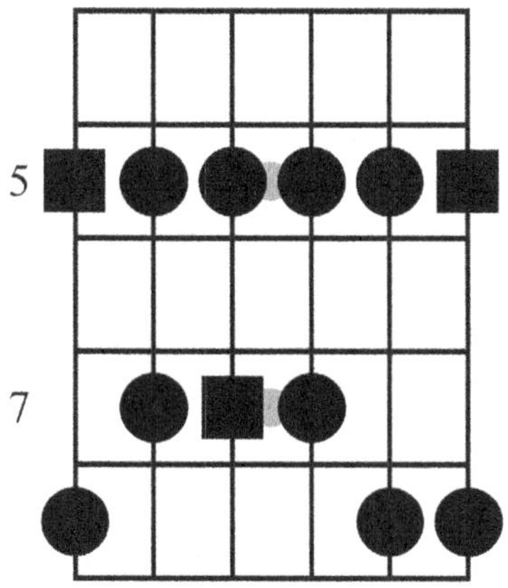

A Minor Pentatonic
Shape 2

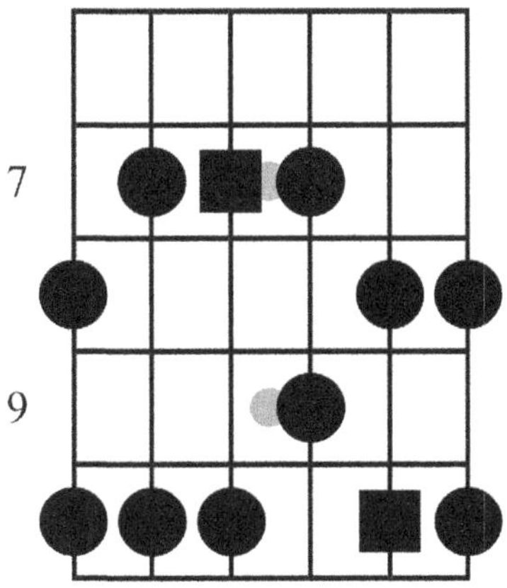

A Minor Pentatonic
Shape 3

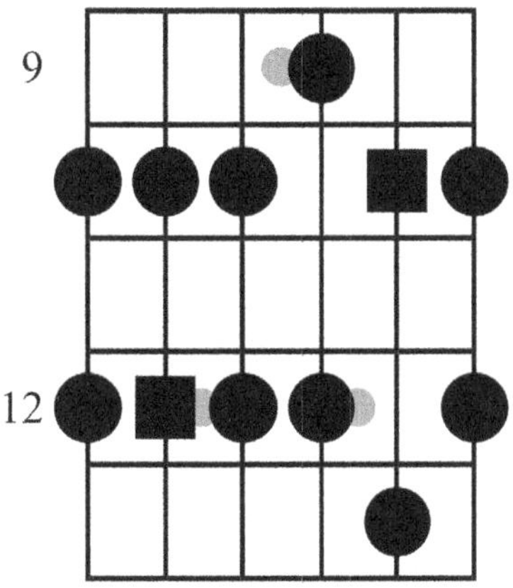

A Minor Pentatonic
Shape 4

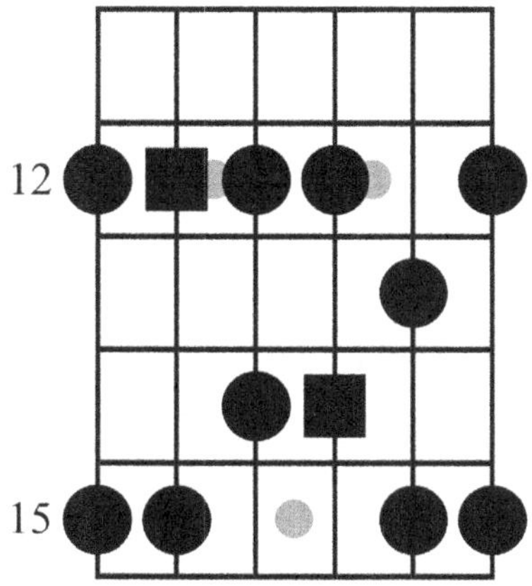

A Minor Pentatonic
Shape 5

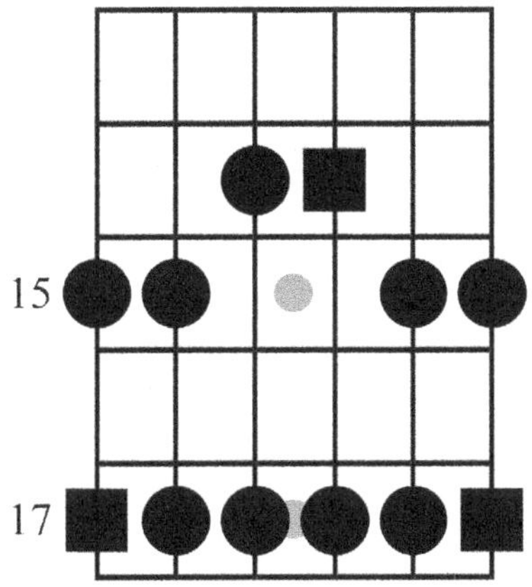

In the licks that follow I'll be using 4ths and 5ths, so let's drill those intervals using Shape 1 of the scale.

First of all, play through A Minor Pentatonic using strict 4ths (i.e. we play the first scale tone, then play the next scale tone a fourth above it, and so on).

Example 6a

We can also play the scale using perfect 4ths intervals (when they are available) and major 3rds (when they're not). When you listen to the audio for this exercise, I think you'll agree that you don't immediately think, "That's minor pentatonic!"

Example 6b

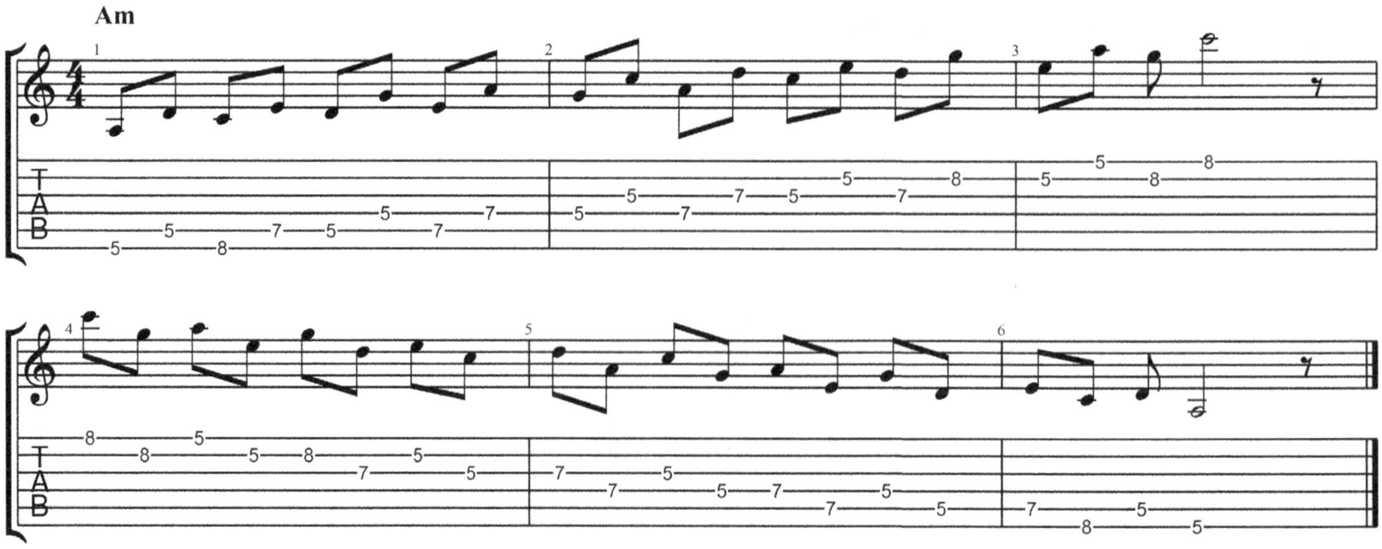

Next, play through Shape 1 of the scale in 5ths. You can, of course, work on applying these interval exercises to all five shapes if you want to nail them.

Example 6c

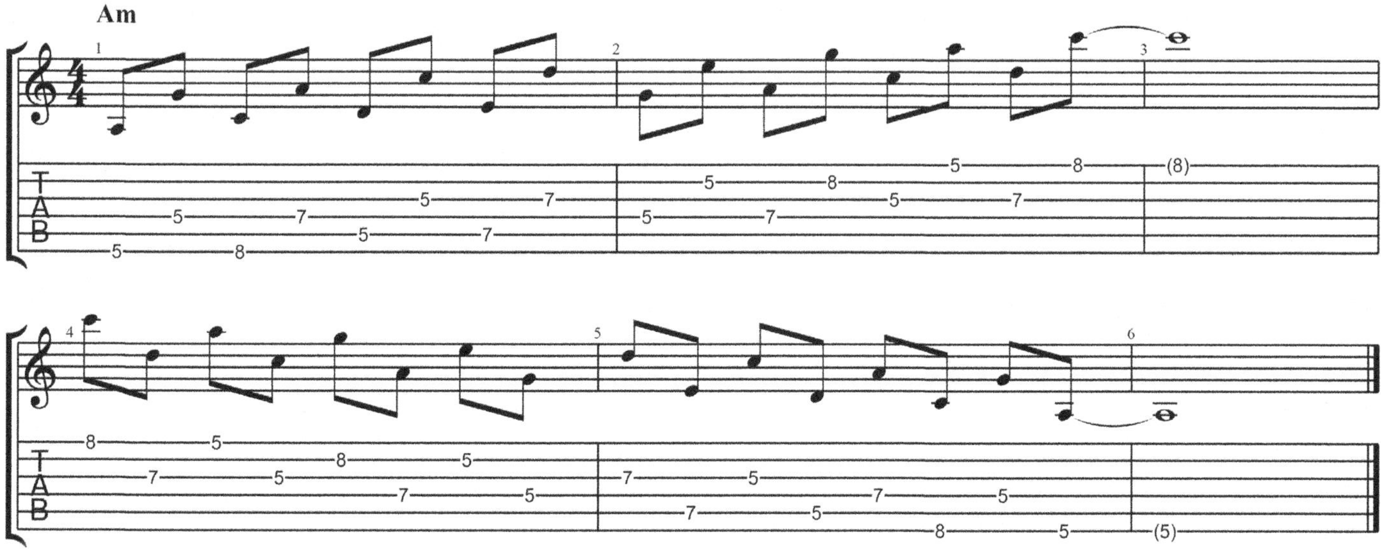

Now let's look at a few of the pentatonic ideas that I use in my playing.

We've already discovered that using wider intervals is a great way to open up your playing and make it less predictable, and this lick achieves that goal with a string skipping idea.

It's based around the familiar Shape 1 of A Minor Pentatonic, but the string skipping helps disguise that fact and gives the line some movement.

It's a scale sequence like you might already play, but it skips a string each time to create some leaps.

In bar two, I precede the half step unison bend at the 7th fret with a fretted C, then bending back to up. The lick ends with a whole step bend to the root.

Example 6d – *Skippit*

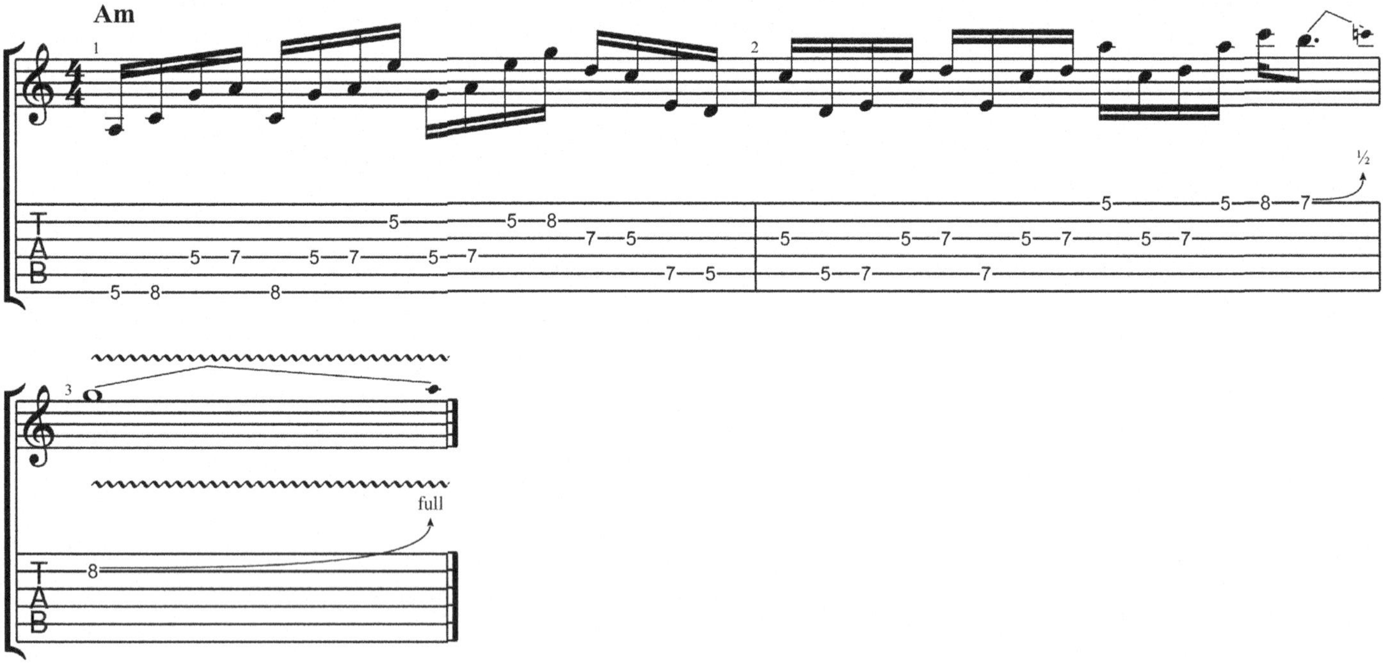

Here's another string skipping idea. This line uses Shape 4 of A Minor Pentatonic, at the 12th fret. I jump strings on the way across, from bottom to top, returning to play one note on the string I omitted.

Then, we have a whole step bend followed by a unison bend, after which the line descends in perfect 4ths and ends with an A minor arpeggio.

Play this line using down-up alternate picking throughout. I also use separate fingers to play this lick, to make it cleaner, apart from in the last phrase where I use a first finger roll for the 4ths at the 12th fret.

Example 6e – *Jumper*

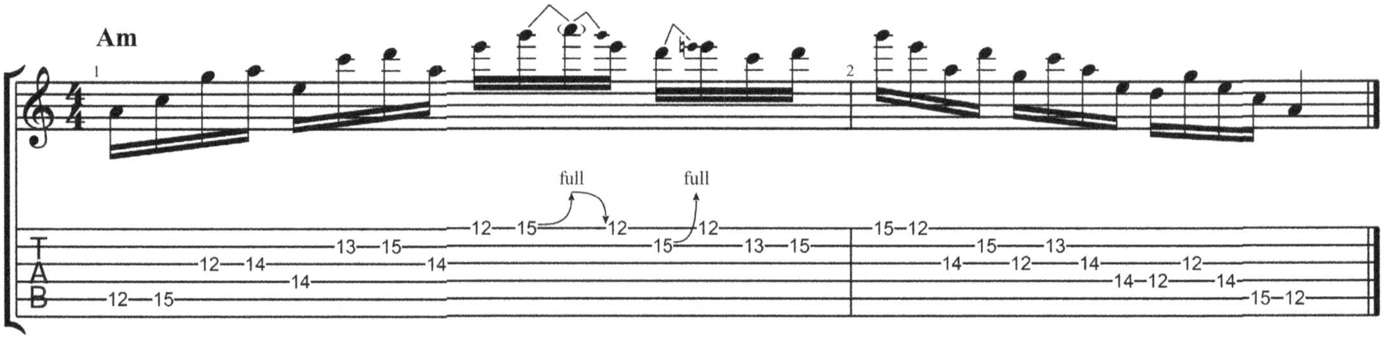

This next lick is built around intervals of a 5th. It descends in 5ths to move across the neck from the top string to the bottom, then I use a series of bends to help climb back up.

This lick uses the Shape 1 pentatonic box that's so familiar to us, but it can be tricky to get the 5ths clean and up to speed. I'm alternate picking this one throughout.

On the way back up there are two half step bends followed by a whole step bend which are all unisons. To end the lick there's another half step bend from F# to G. F# doesn't belong to the A Minor Pentatonic scale – it's just a little outside-inside lick.

Example 6f – *Gimme Five*

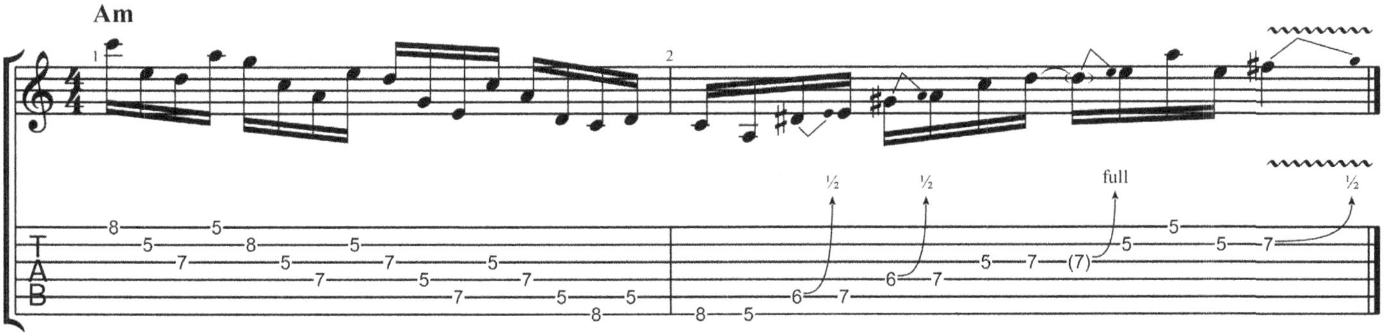

This next lick uses my favorite 1-5-9 shape, and in bar one I use it to move across string sets.

I always play this shape with my first, second and fourth fingers, and though it's a bit of a stretch in the lower register, it's still the best way to fret it.

In the third figure, I break the 1-5-9 shape and play 1-5-1 (like a power chord). Then it's about descending with this same shape.

Often, when I come up with ideas, I see the shapes first and the music comes second. In other words, I'll experiment with a particular shape or pattern of intervals, and if I like the musical results, I'll keep the idea. It's just another creative way of working that helps us to get away from playing predictable scalic runs.

The ending uses perfect 4ths within the pentatonic scale, ending on the root. The first finger of the fretting hand needs to roll (instead of bar) in order to get those clusters of 4ths clean and separated.

This line is trickier to play that it appears on paper, so I recommend walking through it slowly to begin with to ensure that your fingering is economical.

Example 6g – *Symmetry*

Example 6h is a fun lick to play. The descent has a couple of tricky moves where I play 4th intervals in groups of three.

I descend a 4th, then a major third, then I play a series of 4ths on different strings at the same fret.

Rather than rolling a finger, to get it clean, I use separate fingers on each string this time. Also, I keep my fingers in place for this part of the lick, so that I can immediately slide down to the next part with all my fingers correctly aligned.

Next comes an Am7 sweep. I pluck the lead-in G with a pick downstroke, then rake upwards with the pick for the sweep, beginning with hitting the G again.

Some more 4th intervals follow, then another sweep. This time it's a downward swept A minor arpeggio, and the end of the sweep immediately transitions into a half step bend from B to C on the first string, 7th fret.

Example 6h – *Go Sweep the Four*

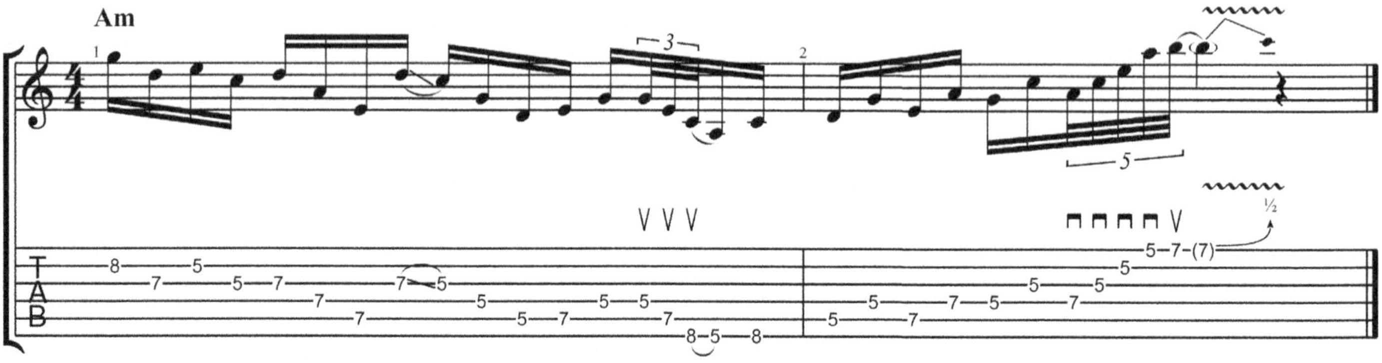

Here's one final pentatonic idea for you.

This one is a little trickier to pull off, with both fretting and picking hands jumping around quite a bit.

You can think of a pentatonic scale as having a left side and a right side, and here I go down the left side in fifth position, all the way from the high E to the low E, then climb up by skipping strings on the right side.

Instead of trying to roll the first finger across the strings here, as it's tempting to do, it's much cleaner to fret each note individually, but this calls for some fretting hand gymnastics. For the opening phrase of bar one, the best approach is to use all four fingers, one per note.

So, you'll play the A on the high E string with the fourth finger, the next note with the third finger, the next note with the second finger, and the final note with the first finger.

Then, you'll start again on the B string and do the same thing, and again from the G string.

It might take a few practices to get this working smoothly, but I promise you it's the best way!

Now we go to the right side of the parallel universe, but here I skip strings. You'll need to adjust your fingering several times for this next part.

Begin with the C on the low E string, 8th fret, in the final group of four notes at the end of bar one. Play the C with your fourth finger and the A with your third.

Next you'll play the E with your second finger and the D with your third.

For the next four-note phrase, which opens bar two, you'll use fingers two and four both times.

Take this slow and rehearse the fingering changes before you launch into the lick.

The line concludes with some bluesy bends and ends on the 4th degree, which lends a kind of suspended feel to the sound.

Example 6i – *Parallel Universe*

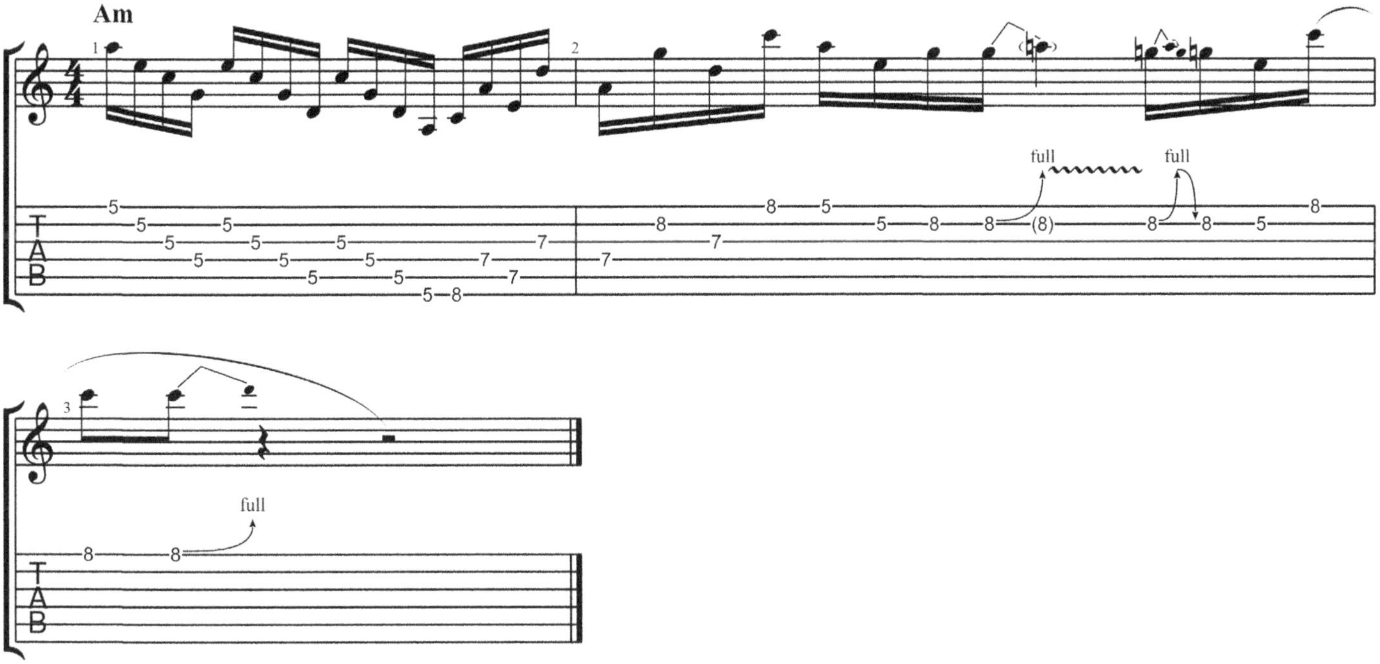

Chapter Seven – Blues Turnaround Licks

In Chapter One we covered a range of licks that you can use over dominant 7 chords. You can transpose those licks to play over any dominant 7 in a different key and, of course, play them in different octaves to get the most out of the material. We know that a typical blues progression is played as three dominant 7 chords, so move those ideas around and you've got some cool intervallic vocabulary to use in a blues setting.

However, it's also worth having some additional melodic vocabulary for the turnaround section of a blues, as it moves from chord V to IV to I in rapid succession – and that's what we'll cover in this chapter as I show you a few of my ideas.

The licks here are for a blues in G Major, so the turnaround sequence is D7 – C7 – G7.

The first lick begins with some 5th intervals over the D7 chord, jumping across the fretboard in ninth position. After the 5ths, you'll hear a standard Rock 'n' Roll movement - a minor 3rd to major 3rd, then 5th to root note.

When the progression changes to C7, you'll find that your fretting hand has crept up one fret to tenth position so keep there for the duration of this bar. This approach forces you to get to know the fretboard better, rather than always moving down a whole step for the IV chord ideas.

The C7 portion is based on diatonic 6th intervals and your hand needs to be pretty spidery for this one. It's a little bit awkward, and you'll need to roll your index finger from the high E string to the G string, to play the fifth and sixth notes of the phrase.

The whole phrase is alternate down-up picked.

Example 7a – *Six to my Stomach*

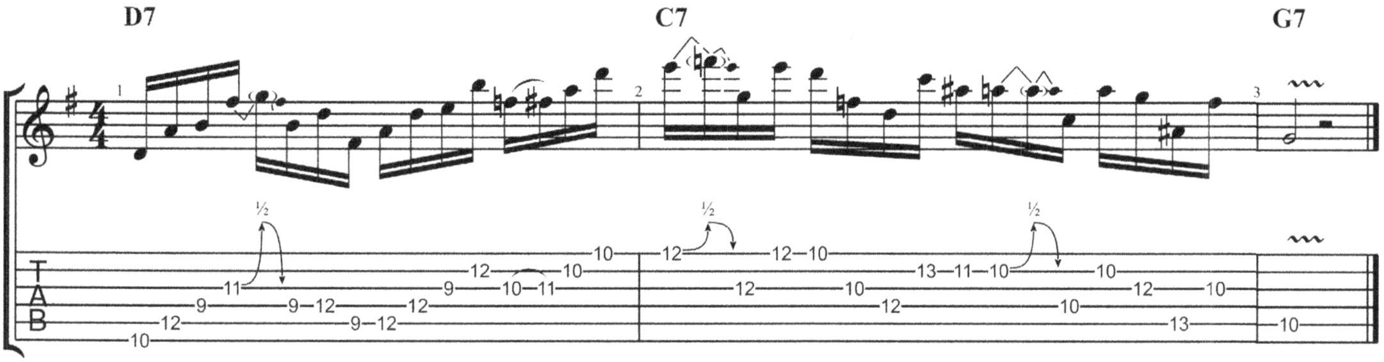

Here's another lick that enables you to stay in one position for both the D7 and C7 chords (because it is *so* tempting to play a lick and just repeat it down a whole step. That idea has its place, but don't overuse it!)

This line has some sweeps at the beginning. In bar one, I start with the 1-5-9 shape beginning on the D root note on the low E string, 10th fret, and have my first, second and fourth fingers hovering over the appropriate frets. The first note is an 1/8th note, and the triplet consists of 1/16th notes. After sweeping the 1-5-9 shape, you'll immediately slide down from the 11th to 9th fret on the G string. This is played with all downstrokes.

The next phrase is a swept D Major triad that transitions into a bend on the high E string. From this position, I stretch out to play a four-note phrase beginning with the C on the B string, 13th fret. This moves to a G# (a passing note that briefly implies the underlying harmony is D7#11), which resolves to A (the 5th of D7). You could also describe it as a b5 to 5 movement. Then the phrase ends on an F# (the 3rd of D7).

Let's look briefly at the first two groups of four notes that kick off bar two, over the C7 chord.

The line begins with a G (the 5th of C7), then the bend pushes a Bb up a whole step to the C root. The F that follows on the high E, 13th fret, is unusual as it's the 11th of the C7 chord and it creates a nice extended sound. The Bb that comes next is the b7.

The second chunk of this phrase contains the notes E, D, A, G – the 3rd, 9th, root and 5th respectively.

It's a great exercise to play a lick in an obvious position for a chord (i.e. tenth position for D7), but then *stay* in that position for the next chord (C7) and see what chord tones you can find there. In this instance, it turns out that several fundamental chord tones are accessible, but also some extended and altered notes.

If you can accommodate a chord change without changing position, chances are that the resulting phrase you play will have great voice leading.

Towards the end of the lick you'll find some diatonic 4ths as well as some smaller scale movements.

Example 7b – *Sweepy the 4th Dwarf*

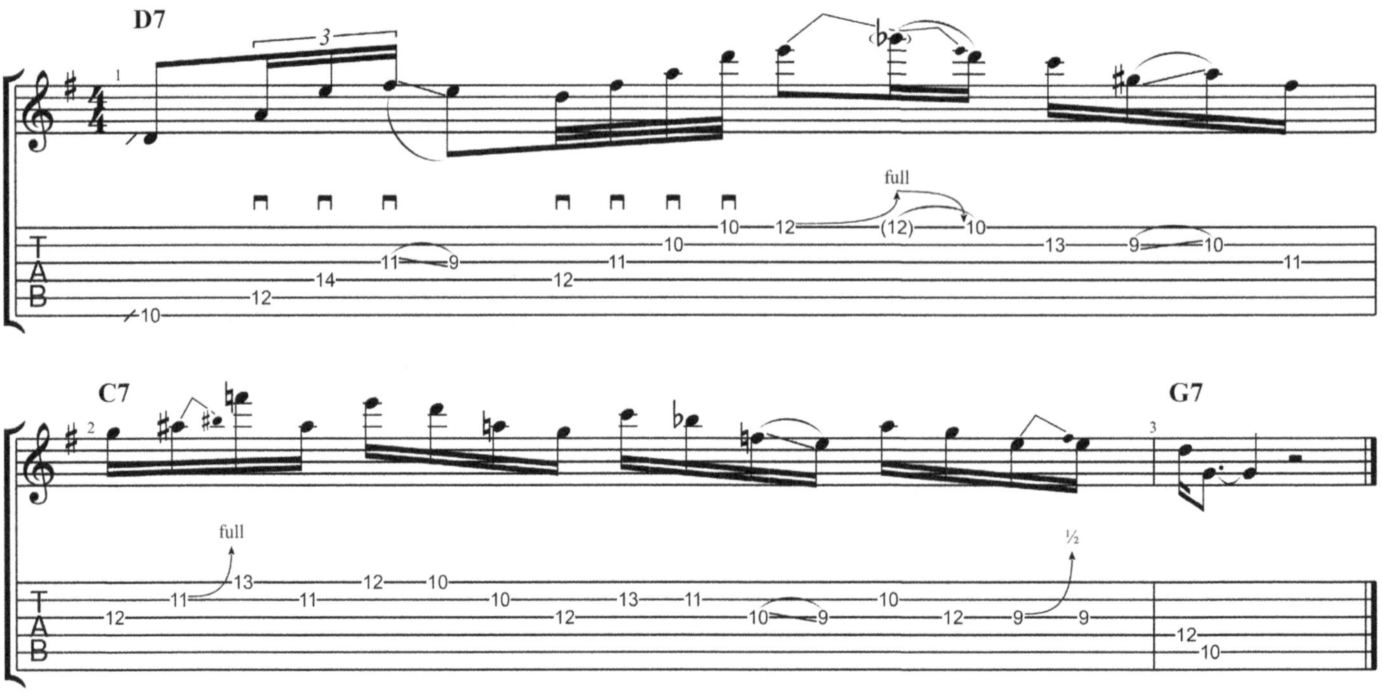

The next lick begins with mostly diatonic 6th intervals over the D7 chord in bar one (with one rogue 5th thrown in for convenience). Rather than play up the scale in 6ths from bottom to top, I change the pattern and move things around a little.

Even large intervals can start to sound predictable if you play them the same way every time. While it's ideal to do this when you're learning them, trying to embed the sound in your ears, in practice it sounds a lot more musical to change things up. You can do this easily by reversing the pattern or adding in slides, bent notes and other articulations.

Another method to keep things interesting is to combine intervals, and as the line in bar one reaches its conclusion, I combine 6ths and 5ths.

As the line continues over the C7 chord in bar two, we have some smaller scalar movements, broken up with whole and half step bends.

Example 7c – *6 Shooter*

This next lick begins with a scalar passage over the D7 chord, which is followed by a line that adds a lot of tension to the C7, mainly through the inclusion of those dissonant b5 intervals that work so well over dominant chords.

After the tension, the release comes in bar three as the lick resolves to the 3rd of the G7. Notice that, again, this lick is based around the same position on the fretboard and accommodates both chords.

Example 7d – *Pay A Tension*

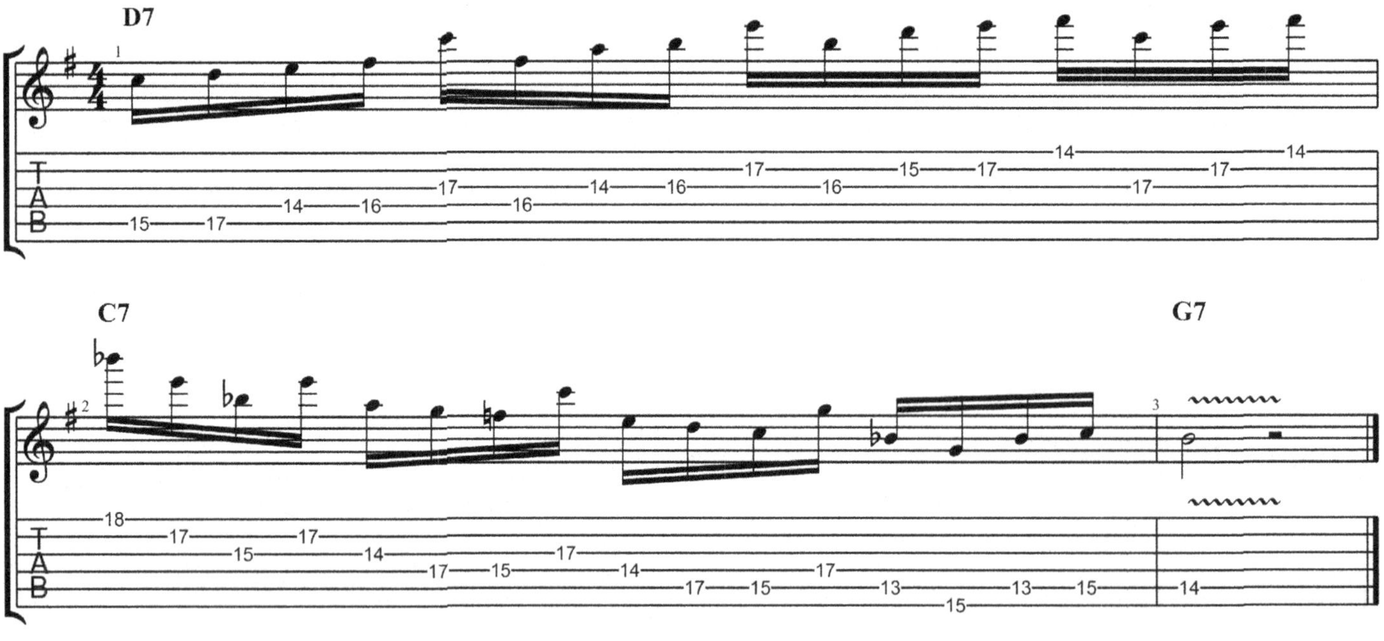

To end this section, here is a tapping lick. It's a little more challenging to play than it sounds on first hearing, as there is some string skipping involved and it requires some tapping with the fourth finger which can take some time to develop if you're not used to it.

For this lick, the fretting hand stays in fifth position throughout. The picking hand goes all the way up to seventeenth position for the higher tapping parts. With both hands spread out over the neck like this, you automatically get wide intervallic jumps, which is what we're aiming for.

As with the previous tapping lick, remember to rest your picking hand thumb on top of the fretboard throughout. It serves as a guide to allow you to slide up and down the neck and fret accurately, and just provides extra stability.

Let me break down the technique I use for tapping/skipping a string here…

In bar one, begin by hammering on with the first finger to the 5th on the A string, and hammer on to the 7th fret with the third finger. Next execute the picking hand tap with the first finger at the 17th fret.

Now, hop your fretting over to the fifth position on the G string and hold it there ready.

Next, you'll play the fretting hand tap on the G string, 17th fret with the second finger. (If you've got your thumb resting on the fretboard, you'll be able to hover your hand in the correct position and maintain its stability). Your second finger now acts as a pick. As you tap, push down toward the floor and away from the string.

From the "picked" tap note, pull off with the fretting hand from the 7th to the 5th fret.

This is the essence of the technique needed to execute the whole lick. It's a matter of getting your hands coordinated and working together smoothly. Walk through the movements slowly until you've locked the hand interaction into muscle memory.

Example 7e – *12 Foot Spread*

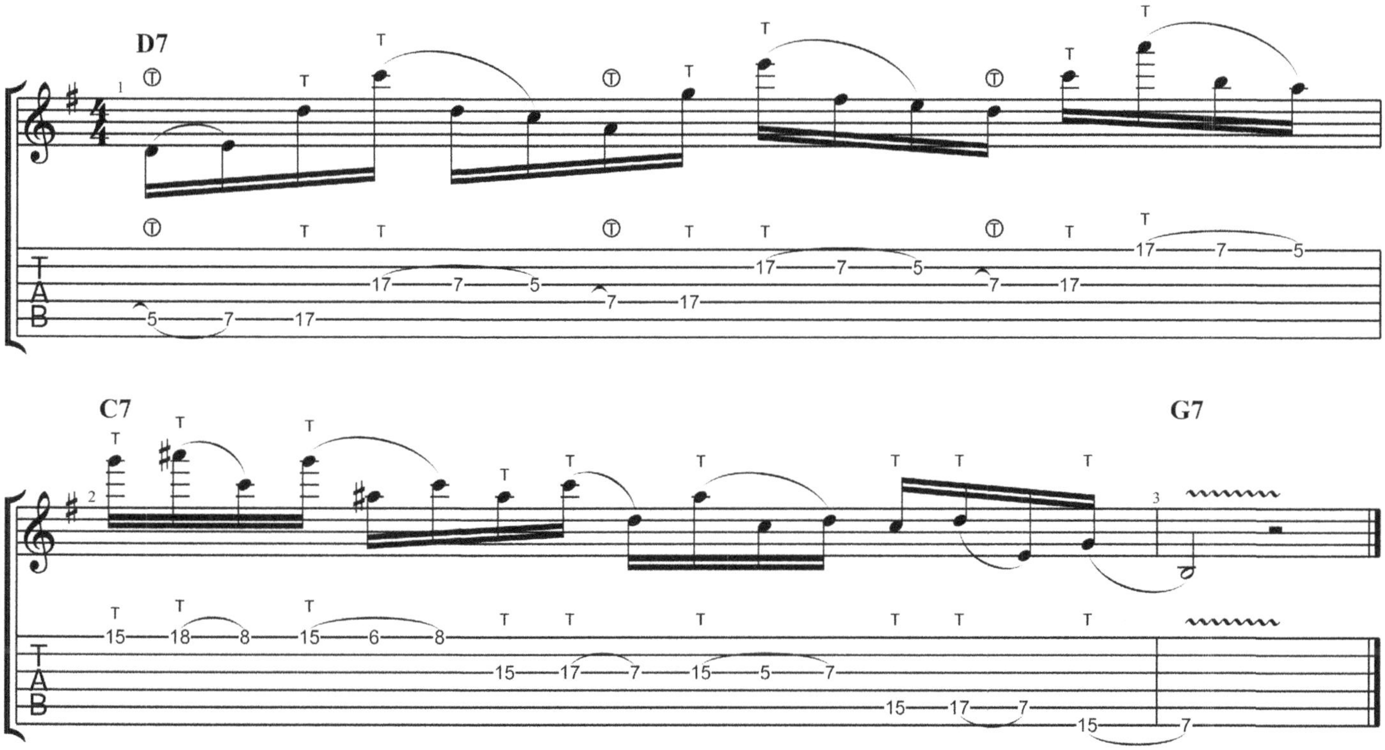

Chapter Eight – Altered Dominant Licks

In this final chapter, I wanted to share some of the lick vocabulary I use over altered dominant chords that have at least one, but sometimes multiple alterations to a basic "7" chord.

Often on a chord chart you'll see some unfathomable chord such as the one in Example 8a (E7b9#5) and you may think, "What the heck should I play over that?"

One approach is to know all the chord tones of a standard E7 chord, and to think in terms of adding tension notes to an E7 arpeggio.

An E7 chord contains the notes E, G#, B, D

If we then incorporate an F, for example, into our arpeggio pattern, we create an E7b9 sound.

This approach can work well for some people, but it can also get complicated quickly, and the more you are having to think about what you're playing, the less musical it will sound.

There are three other strategies that I like to use that are simpler to apply and get the same results.

1. Using the Whole Tone scale. Playing the Whole Tone over an altered dominant chord will naturally bring out all of those altered tension notes. We'll see how in just a moment. This is my number one approach, and most of the licks in this chapter use it.
2. A second approach is to mix and match scales relating to the tonal center. Over E7, for example, I might mix and match E Mixolydian, E Minor Pentatonic and E Major scales. These each have a number of notes in common, but they also have their differences, and these differences suggest certain tensions over an E7 chord.
3. Lastly, I've already mentioned that I'm a fan of moving shapes around on the fretboard and seeing what the result is. I'll also use the simple technique of side-stepping to create altered tensions i.e. playing a shape constructed from diatonic notes and shifting it up or down a half step. The results can be surprising.

Before we explore some licks, let's get familiar with the E Whole Tone.

About the Whole Tone scale

The Whole Tone is a *hexatonic* scale, meaning that it has only six notes per octave. The name of the scale explains exactly what it is – a series of pitches each a *whole tone* (two frets) apart.

It has been used in Rock guitar playing, but also in Classical music and Jazz (especially by musicians such as John Coltrane, Wayne Shorter and McCoy Tyner). Because of its entirely whole step construction, it's a great scale for creating tension because it never sounds as though it resolves.

Over the E7alt chord vamp we'll play the E Whole Tone scale.

E Whole Tone contains the notes: E, F#, G#, A#, C, D

The great thing about an altered scale is that it does a lot of the hard work for you. Played over a straight E7 chord, the notes of E Whole Tone automatically create the following tensions:

E	F#	G#	A# / Bb	C	D
Root	9th	3rd	#11 / b5	#5	b7

Now let's take a look at the A and E string root shapes for playing the E Whole Tone scale.

Due to the unique nature of the Whole Tone's construction, it falls on the fretboard as a combination of two- and three-notes-per-string.

First, here is the A string root pattern, based around seventh position. I've added the scale tones on the low E string as hollow notes to complete the pattern but learn the scale from the root.

E Whole Tone scale

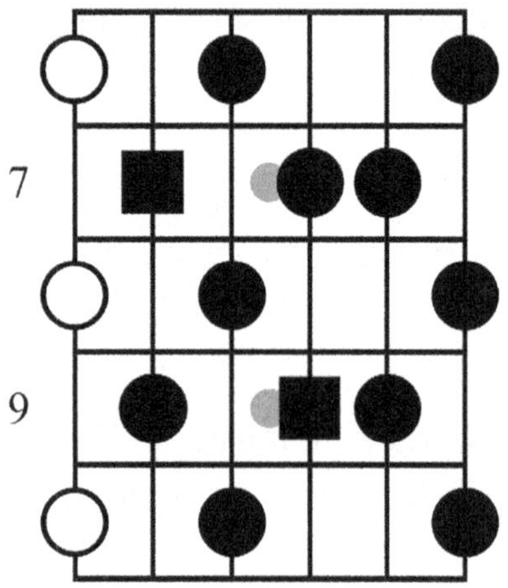

And here is the E string root pattern in twelfth position. You can also play this in the lower register, of course, incorporating the open strings.

E Whole Tone scale

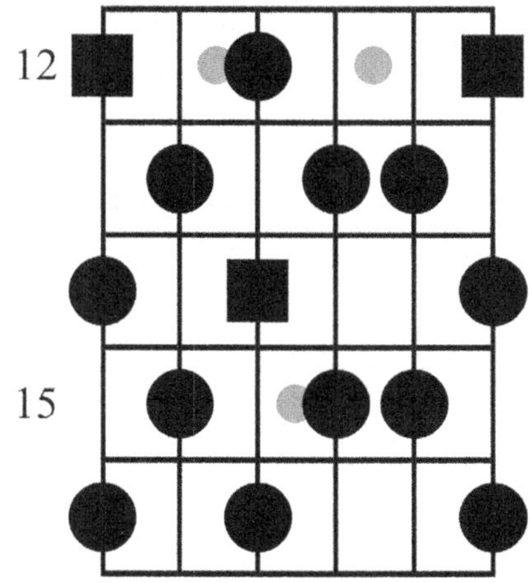

If you prefer, you can also play the E string root shape this way, beginning with two notes on the low E string, rather than three.

E Whole Tone scale

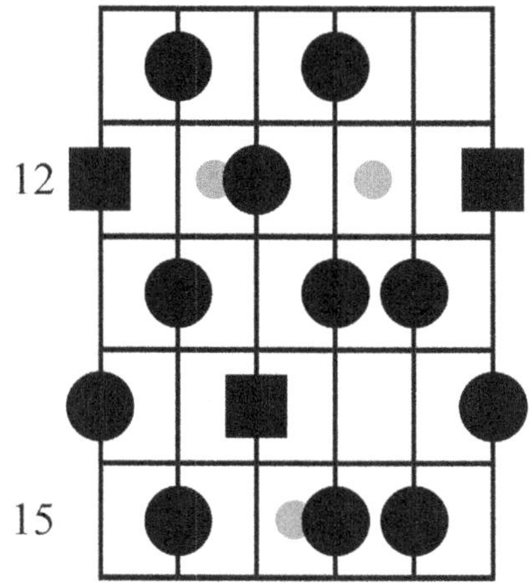

Drill these shapes in your practice times to get them under your fingers. It's hard to get lost playing the Whole Tone, because the next note is always a whole step away! The difficult part is getting it to sound musical, but this can be achieved with a bit of practice and produce wonderful results.

Now let's get into the licks.

This first lick is based around the E Whole Tone scale but with a couple of passing note additions that further spice up the tension.

I add in an F, which implies an E7b9 sound and there's also a D# thrown in. The latter is the major 7th (rather than the b7 of E7), but here I'm just viewing it as a chromatic approach note that leads to the E that follows.

Note that, you don't have to wait until you see a chord chart with this exact chord written down before you use this lick. You can play it over a straight E7 chord to add tension. If you do, however, be sure to resolve the tension, otherwise people will laugh and point – and that's not good!

Example 8a – *Stairs of Escher*

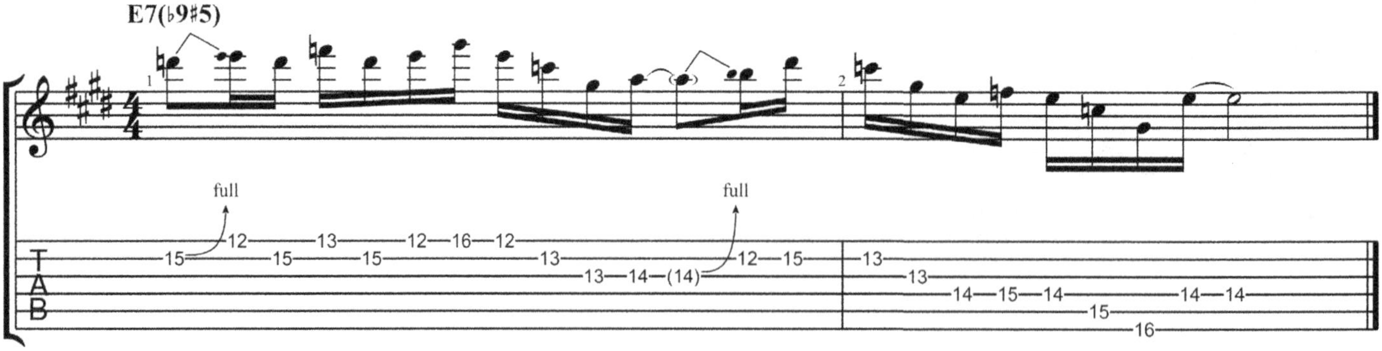

The next lick is an example of how side-stepping a simple shape can work effectively to create tension.

At the beginning of this lick I play a root to 3rd to 6th movement using the notes of the E Major scale (E, G#, C#). Then I move up a half step and play the same pattern, but in reverse.

In relation to the E7 chord, the side-stepped notes (D, A, F) are the b7, 11th and b9. The side-step worked out pretty well! It may not always, but it's worth experimenting with this idea to create new sounds from simple patterns.

The next part of the lick is a simple E Major triad with the 5th as the lowest note.

Next I hop over a string and play similar notes to the earlier side-stepped phrase. Here it's F (b9), A (11th) and B (5th). The result of this little shape over the E groove is to create an Esusb9 sound.

At the end, I bend the b7 degree up a minor third to reach the b9 and finally re-bend the same note a whole step, resolving on the root.

This lick creates the overall sound of an E7b9#5 when played over an E7 chord.

Example 8b – *Fall Down*

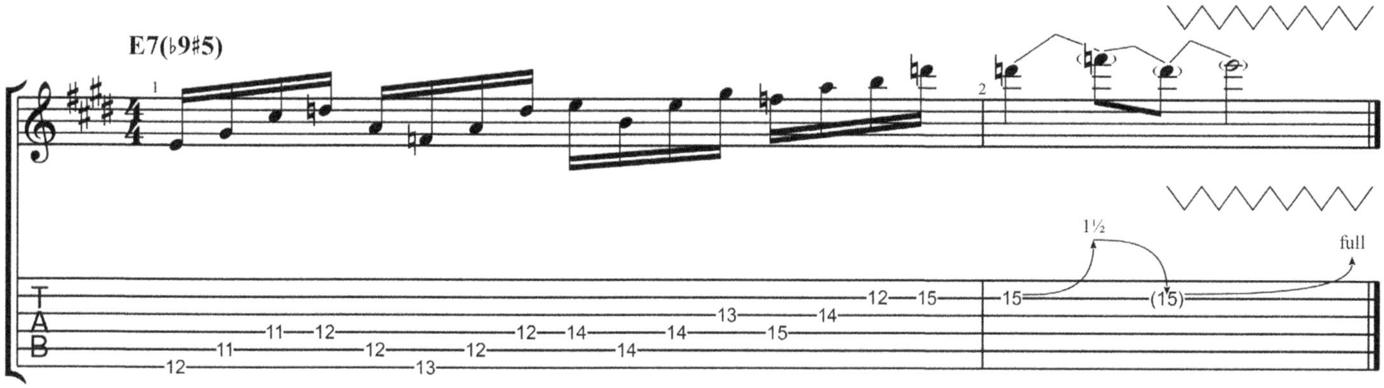

I called the next lick *Purple Maze* because it reminds me of Jimi Hendrix who is synonymous with that dominant 7#9 sound, and especially in the track *Purple Haze.*

Here, I use a strategy of combining scales based around the tonal center. I use E Minor Pentatonic and E Mixolydian ideas. The result is that the lick has both minor and major 3rds in it and gives us the minor/major combination that's so often found in the blues.

The aim of this lick was to include some perfect 4th intervals and end by targeting the #9 of the E7 chord.

Example 8c – *Purple Maze*

We're back to the Whole Tone scale for the next lick.

Playing E Whole Tone over an E7 chord enables us to easily access the b5 and #5 tension notes. A benefit of this scale is that, since it's organized entirely in whole steps, you can play a whole step bend on any scale tone and automatically land on another sale tone. So, this lick is a descending idea that punctuates the run with several whole step bends.

In bar one, I kick off with a whole step bend on the first string, quickly followed by another on the second string. Next, there are some string jumps using 6th intervals, another whole step bend, then more 6ths.

From there I walk down the Whole Tone scale to land on the root.

Example 8d – *Wholey Moley*

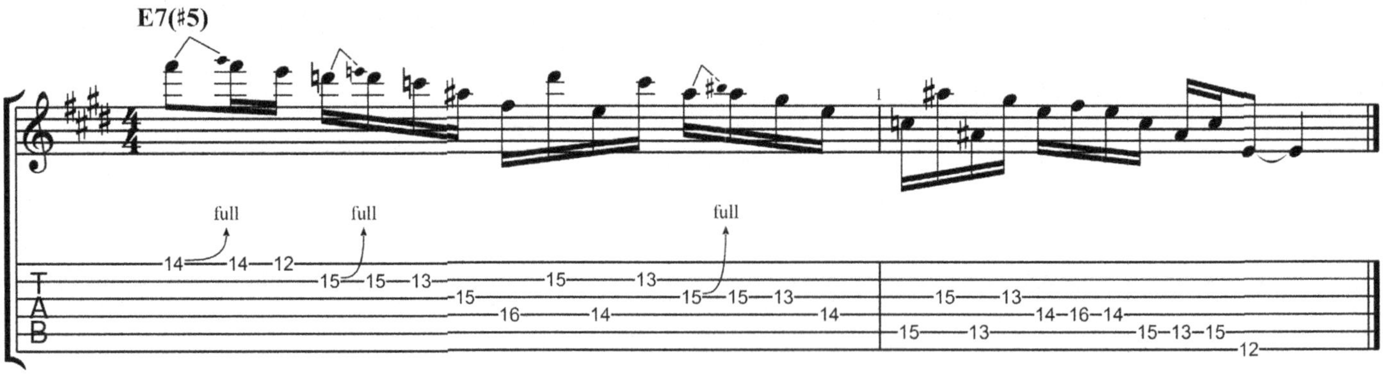

Here's an example of using the Whole Tone scale in a tapping lick. I focus on playing b5 intervals in both hands for this one, so it's a pretty tense sounding line.

If you've not done a whole lot of tapping in your playing, you might find it tricky to control your picking hand taps, as it requires the use of multiple fingers. But fear not, I will walk you through how to approach it!

First, fret the E at the 12th fret on low E string, with your index finger.

Now, assign one finger per fret and allow your other fingers to form a diagonal pattern across the next three strings. (Your second finger will be on the A string, 13th fret; the third finger on the D string, 14th fret; the fourth finger on the G string, 15th fret).

This is the shape your fretting hand will hold throughout the entire lick, and those are the strings/notes your fingers are assigned to.

The picking hand mirrors this *exact same shape*, starting with the first finger assigned to the 18th fret. You'll use all four fingers of the picking hand, which means the fourth finger will be tapping on the 21st fret on the third string.

The picking hand is playing in the top register of the guitar where the frets are closer together, so tapping accuracy is all important to get a good sound. There's a lot going on here, so spend some time rehearsing your hand coordination.

Remember to keep your thumb resting on top of the fingerboard to help with stability and accuracy.

Example 8e – Whole Tone Jones

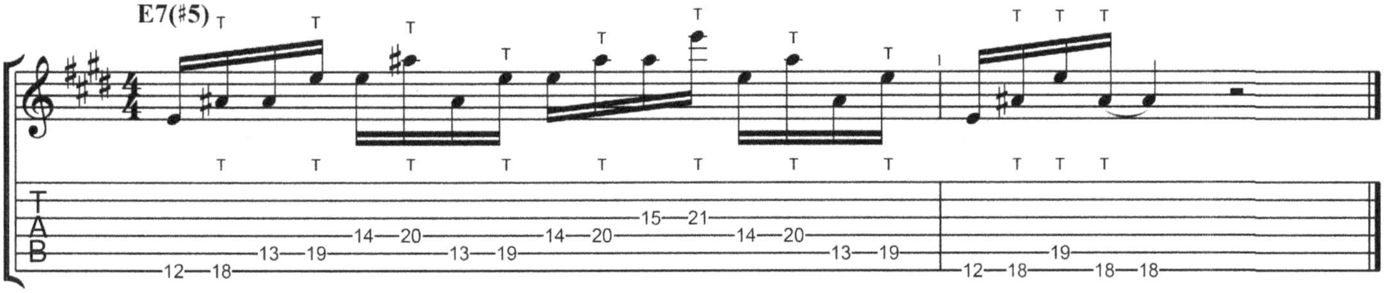

Here's another Whole Tone tapping lick – this time it's a cascading line with the notes arranged in groups of six.

For this one, I use the first and third fingers of the fretting hand for the lower tapped notes, and the same fingers of the picking hand for the higher tapped notes.

I also use the picking hand first finger like a pick here, to sound the first note in the pickup bar.

The lick is made up of all whole tone steps. After the two lead-in notes in the pickup bar, it's all about descending in six-note groupings and keeping that cascading momentum going.

Notice that the last note of each group of six always falls on the next string down. Practice this lick by initially isolating each group of six, treating it as an individual phrase, then connect all the phrases together at the end.

Example 8f – *Fresh Air*

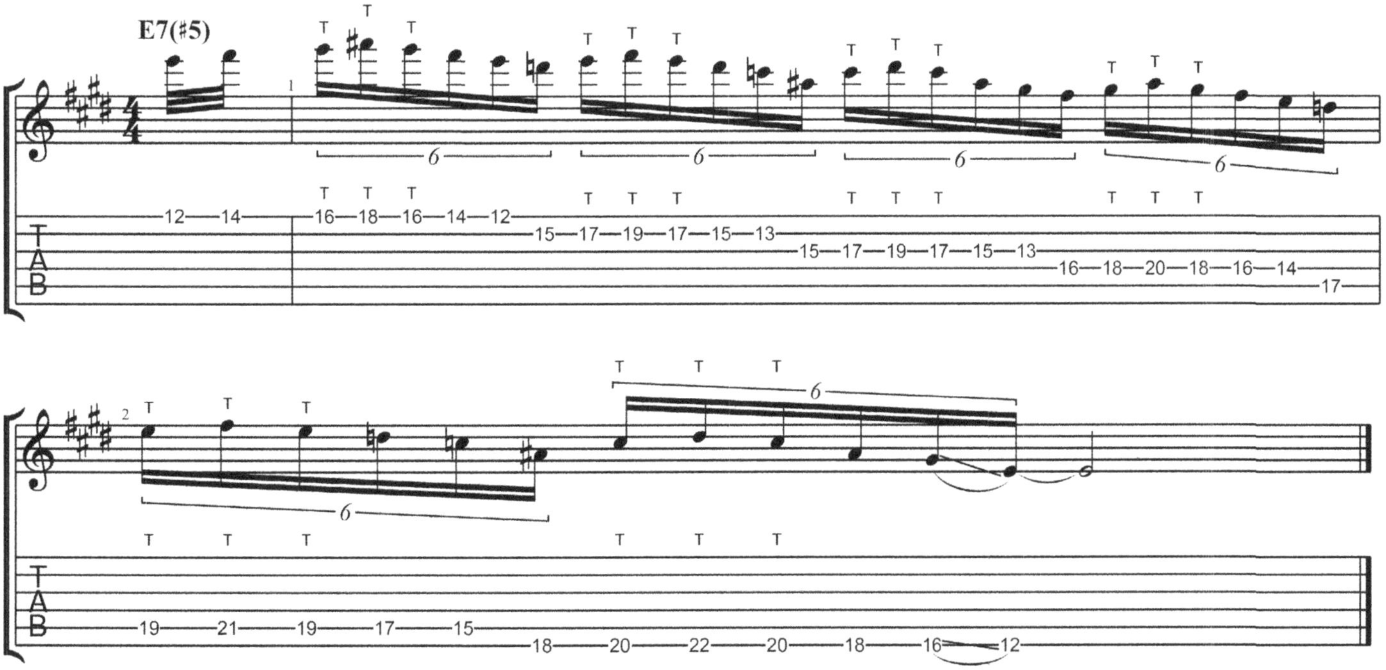

To wrap things up, here's another Whole Tone descending line that includes some whole step bends.

For the opening bend, I use a downward pick stroke to start the bend, then pick downward again when it's released, followed by an upstroke. This picking pattern is repeated on the adjacent string as the line begins to descend. On the third string, however, you need to reverse the pattern and play *up-down-up* because of where this phrase falls in the bar.

Then there is a short sequence of three Whole Tone scale steps which is repeated a b5 below the original. I end the line on the 3rd of E7 after bending that tone up a whole step and releasing it.

Over an E7, this line gives you both the b5 and #5 sounds. This lick also works well on the V chord of a blues turnaround.

Example 8g – *Prince of Wholes*

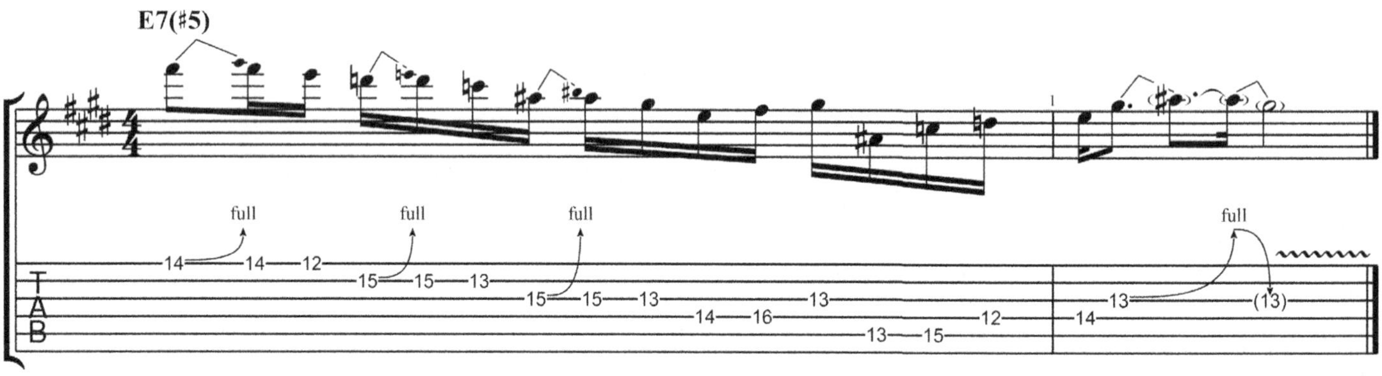

Conclusion

Thank you for working your way through this collection of intervallic licks. I hope you got a lot out of the material contained here. I love using intervals to get away from the predictable stuff we can all fall into at times. Thinking intervallically, rather than scalically, can open up a whole vista of new ideas and help you move forward as a player.

To continue to develop these ideas for yourself, make time for some interval workouts in your practice sessions. You can refer to the exercises at the beginning of each chapter that walk you through scales in different intervals, or you can invent your own.

The main thing is to embed the sound of each interval in your ears, and to work on visualizing them on the fretboard. That way, you'll naturally begin to play more intervallic lines and include them as part of your unique sound.

Don't forget to have fun with it along the way!

If you want to find out more about what I'm up to currently, stop by **www.jenniferbatten.com** for a visit.

Jennifer.

Made in United States
North Haven, CT
27 January 2023

31564104R00046